M000003815

CLUB GRANDMA

Etiquette, Privileges & Official Duties

by
Leslie Lehr Spirson
with
Claire J. Lehr, Ph.D.

Longmeadow Press

For Juliette & Catherine
and
All the Members of Club Grandma:
Enjoy the Children!

Copyright © 1994 by Leslie Lehr Spirson

Published by Longmeadow Press, 201 High
Ridge Road, Stamford, CT 06904. All rights
reserved. No part of this book may be repro-
duced or utilized in any form or by any means,
electronic or mechanical, including photocopy-
ing, recording or by any information storage and
retrieval system, without permission in writing
from the Publisher.

Longmeadow Press and the colophon are
registered trademarks.

Cover design by Kelvin P. Oden
Interior design by Allan Mogel
Library of Congress Cataloging-in-Publication Data

Spirson, Leslie Lehr.
    Club grandma : etiquette, privileges & official duties / by Leslie
Lehr Spirson with Claire J. Lehr — 1st ed.
        p.   cm.
    1. Grandmothers—Humor.   2. Grandparenting—Humor.   I. Lehr,
Claire J.
HQ759.9.S7   1994
306.874′5—dc20   93-37299
                                                               CIP
ISBN: 0-681-45323-0
Printed in United States of America
First Edition
0 9 8 7 6 5 4 3 2 1

Contents

1.

* * * * * *

Welcome to Club Grandma!

How old are your grandchildren?"
"Well, the doctor's two and the lawyer's four.
—Anonymous

Congratulations! It's time to reap the rewards of motherhood. Time to feel special and wonderful and beautiful and proud. Time to fall in love again. The work is over—now the fun begins!

Have you been eyeing baby clothes for years? Or did the news take you completely by surprise? Were you shocked at the vision of your son as a father? Did you give not-so-subtle hints to your daughter? Maybe you were looking forward to the announcement, but when it came, you were secretly anxious. You're not alone. In fact, even if you have a closet full of pink and blue Sleep'n Plays, it's natural to be a little bit nervous. After all, grandchildren are living proof that your children are getting older. Luckily, being a grandmother is one of the most rewarding roles you'll ever have.

It takes years for your own children to grow from infancy to adulthood. No matter how many years lie in between, you've still got the majority of your life left over—as a grandmother. For the first time in history, women can enjoy an average of forty years of grandparenting. Just when you're feeling the mid-life blahs a precious gift is given to you . . . a baby to love and spoil, then give back to the parents!

Noted scholars, artists and athletes attest to the special relationship between a child and a grandmother:

- Anthropologist Margaret Mead believed that her paternal grandmother was "the most decisive influence" in her life.

5

- Supreme Court Justice Sandra Day O'Connor spent several formative years living with her grandmother, the legendary Mamie Wilkey, who led a wagon train across the Sierra Madre.
- Olympic diver Mark Lenzi dedicated his gold medal to his grandmother, who died before the 1992 Olympic Games.
- Governor Ann Richards of Texas attributes her political goals to her overwhelming love for her granddaughter Lily.
- Oscar-winning actor Al Pacino relied on his grandmother for inspiration following his parents' divorce when he was two years old.
- Singer Rosemary Clooney dedicated the song, "Our Love Is Here To Stay," to her four grandchildren during a Fourth of July Hollywood Bowl performance.

The list goes on. You too, can make a difference in your grandchildren's lives—and you can have fun doing it!

You can't choose to be a grandmother. You can, however, choose what kind of grandmother to be. Suddenly, those nine long months are up, and you are biologically connected to a brand new person. As a grandparent, you can explore the world from a fresh perspective, nurture and influence the future, and enjoy a wonderful relationship with a child who wants to love you forever. Take advantage of the happiness ahead. Learn how to be a "great" grandma.

You know you're a member of Club Grandma when . . .

— the clerk at the toy store knows you by name.
— your children ask you for advice.
— you judge a country club by the size of the swimming pool.
— you realize that "Rock-A-Bye Baby" is not a nice song.
— you think it's adorable when young children are on the answering machine message.

2.

⊛ ⊛ ⊛ ⊛ ⊛ ⊛ ⊛

Initiation

*Perfect love sometimes does not come
until the first grandchild.*
—Welsh Proverb

The First Grandchild

I'll bet you'll always remember exactly where you were when you first became a grandmother. I know my mother will—she was with me. The awe of creation ignited a rebirth of our relationship. We shared an unforgettable experience.

Nana's Story:

The call came first thing in the morning. My son-in-law said, "You're going to be a grandmother—soon!" Chills went down my spine.

"Are you serious? How is she? Oh my God, I've got to pack!" I rushed around throwing my things into an overnight bag. It was ten days before she was due. I wasn't ready. The hospital was in Santa Monica—I lived in Orange County, an hour and a half away.

If the drivers next to me on the freeway were listening, they would have heard classical music on full blast. My grandchild was going to be born into the world in style.

My Story

I waited as long as I could before letting my husband call my mother. I was excited to have her there, yet I felt possessive about the experience belonging only to us.

> *Proudly I entered St. John's Hospital. I raced to the elevator. As I turned the corner coming out, there was Leslie pacing the corridor with the huge baby in her belly. And there was Jon helping her. Leslie saw me. With her tears, she looked like the baby she had been, years ago. I was elated and frightened all at once. This was it. Real Life.*

I didn't mean to cry—I didn't want to cry—but when I saw my mother, I just couldn't help it. I was so relieved that she had made it. Like many mothers and daughters, we've had a rocky relationship, but now we had motherhood in common. The next contraction reminded me that she went through all this pain for me once. I was grateful.

> *The birthing room was scary—like a normal hotel room but with tubes and monitors all over the place . . . it reminded me of "Star Trek." The parents-to-be had brought lots of cassette tapes. I have absolutely no idea what music I heard, even though it played all day and most of the night. At one point we turned on the television and watched bits of "All My Children." Leslie was in a lot of pain. I don't know why they didn't give her more medication. I didn't like that natural childbirth stuff. When I had her, they knocked me right out. It was civilized. I pulled out a new book of short stories and started reading out loud.*

My mother badgered the nurses so much I would have been horrified if I hadn't been in so much pain. I was embarrassed

9

to ask for drugs so I waited until I couldn't bear it. By the time the nurses got it together, all the shot did was make a red dot on my rear. They wouldn't give me the epidural until I was farther along. I felt like I was sitting on a gas stove and somebody kept jacking up the flame. My husband was watching the monitor and tried to pacify me once by saying the contraction was only a mild one, but the monitor lied and I let him know it. Mom just watched cheerfully and made small talk. She was as nervous as she was at my wedding. I felt like a wild animal thrashing about.

At some point, Mom pulled out a book and started reading short stories. I thought she was out of her mind . . . then the stories got interesting. She had to start over when each contraction interrupted, but it turned out to be a wonderful distraction.

It did occur to me that my presence might seem strange to married grandparents. As a divorced mother, those years of struggle and emotional pain had formed an invincible bond between us. I felt like part of the coaching team. The beautiful couple in front of me brought me back to the present. I started crying again.

We had decided on a girl's first name but that was about it. It's amazing that you have all those months to pick names and it's still so impossible. My husband blurted out that we would name a girl Juliette Claire, with the middle name after my mother. We hadn't agreed on this, but he pretty much ended the discussion right there. I wasn't up to an argument and we couldn't exactly take it back. My Mom was so overjoyed, you'd think it never crossed her mind. I realized it was a good thing—this baby would never be lacking in the grandma department.

I said, "It doesn't matter if it's a girl or a boy, as long as it's healthy." But, I couldn't help it. I was seduced. I wanted a girl.

Finally, early the next morning, it was time. Worn out, I left the special event to the Spirson team. A few minutes later, I heard a baby cry. Then, they invited me back in and I saw her. Juliette Claire was the most incredible baby in all the world. I was part of it all. And she was part of me.

The Universal Response to the News

Q: **What do you say when you hear the news?**
A: *I'm going to be a Matriarch!*

No matter what your immediate thoughts are about becoming a grandmother, once the reality sinks in, instinct takes over. Your baby is going to have a baby. Seems like yesterday, you were the one changing diapers.

Your Baby

The first thing my mother did was typical of all new grandmothers. She dug out the family scrapbook and bored everyone who dared step foot in her home. Then, she started sending me faded old photographs in the mail. Did this prove that I was cute or just that she really was a mother, way back when? Either way, now I have dozens of ancient pictures shoved in my albums at random; she's got a book with a lot of empty, faded squares. It was a natural response, though, so I tried to be understanding.

Initiation

• • • • •

Your new parents will try to be understanding too . . . until you start sending child development books by the caseload. In a few short weeks, I amassed a full library of baby books, child psychology tomes and medical texts. Suddenly, I had subscriptions to half a dozen parenting magazines. She sent nursery rhyme anthologies, in case I forgot. She even threw in a children's dictionary, for future reference. Finally, when it was time for a new bookcase, I called her on the phone.

"So, Mom, hey, thanks for the books."

"Oh, did you get them?" she sounded nonchalant.

"I sure did. All of them. I mean, I hope it's all of them. The UPS man swears whenever he sees me. He's getting a hernia."

"That's crude, honey."

"Sorry. So, tell me the truth . . . you don't think I'll be a good mother?"

That did it. The dam broke. She sobbed. "That's not it. I just never taught you how!"

"It's not like there's a test, Mom. So far as I know, they just hand you the baby in the hospital, no license or anything."

"Well, there should be something. It's the most important thing you'll ever do. You didn't even like to baby-sit!"

"That's because our neighbor's daughter was a brat."

"I just want you to be prepared. It's a big job, you know."

"I know Mom, but I can always call you for help, right?"

It's natural to be concerned. Give your children as much information as possible. Then trust biology for that maternal instinct to kick in. And keep an open telephone line!

Connecting the Past with the Future

Suddenly, I was being regaled with stories about my great grandparents. I know Mom was enjoying her ride down memory lane, and it was pretty interesting, so I just listened. After a few weeks, I realized she was savoring memories as a method of gathering research. She was building a model of the perfect grandma in her mind. We're talking half a century ago, and somehow I knew my mother would never grow her hair to the floor and wear it wrapped up in a braid. Hey, she's a California blonde! I also knew she wouldn't be luring the children to the kitchen with the aroma of fresh-baked sweets. I was confident that she'd keep a cupboard full of Cheerios and hit the Chinese takeout place regularly.

Then, she started collecting family histories. With a psychotherapist for a mother, I'm used to having my family and friends dissected on a regular basis. But now, she wasn't just fooling around with idle research. She was examining patterns of parenting to see how my husband and I would stack up. It was scary.

Next, she started planning the financial strategy necessary to buy her grandchild a pony. She planned sightseeing trips around the world. She took seminars on college tuition planning. Unless she won the lottery, most of these plans were a bit unrealistic, but it was the thought that counted.

Finally, we started playing the name game. Everywhere she went, my mother asked people their full names. She watched the credits roll on every movie and television show and took notes in case she found the perfect name. She called me whenever she heard a new one. This was fun for a while, but there came the time when I was ready to call the kid Bozo the Clown just to end the discussion.

At that point I knew my mother would need a bigger handbag for her baby pictures. I mean, I was excited, but I also had heartburn, varicose veins, bags under my eyes and an embarrassingly weak bladder. She was happy, healthy and wild with anticipation. I heard about the new baby store in her neighborhood before the news about her credit card being stolen. Overwhelming excitement is natural, and it doesn't go away—not for the second grandchild or the third, or even, as many grandmothers have told me, the fifteenth. Each baby is another jewel in your crown.

Pride that your bloodline will extend into the future brings a sense of immortality. After all, what the world really needs is more of you, right? A woman's eggs are formed while she is a fetus in her mother's belly. So, if you have a daughter, her children are definitely made of your stuff. Your imprint will be on this Earth for decades, if not centuries, to come. Immortality is even more clear when you have a son and the family name—as well as your blood—lives on.

It's not just blood, however, that determines ancestry. If your children or grandchildren are adopted, your influence has profound significance. Your grandchildren may pick up your sense of humor or your loyalty or your zest for life. They will certainly blossom from your spiritual gifts and in turn, they will pass them on to the next generation. Grandchildren are a magic potion that lets you live forever.

The Baby Shower

The importance of this event cannot be stressed. Sure, it's an excuse to get presents, but more than that, it's a show of support. If the new mother's friends haven't made solid plans by the fifth month, step right up! The baby shower can be a potluck picnic, a formal tea or a buffet brunch. It can be in your home, at a restaurant, or at the guest-of-honor's house. If need be, you can plan it from across the country: request a list of names and addresses, mail the invitations, pick up party supplies and be there a day ahead to prepare.

When I had my first baby, I didn't know any other mothers, so my mother and I did it ourselves. Mom cooked her delicious seafood casserole, I made Chinese chicken salad and my sister flew down in time to ball honeydew into a scooped out watermelon. My husband helped decorate, then escaped to the movies. It was an awful lot of work, and we probably could have bought all the gifts ourselves just as easily. Nevertheless, it was fun and it meant a lot to my mother and sister and I at the start of a newly defined relationship.

By the time my second child made her appearance, several of my new "Mommy" friends pitched in to share a baby sitter and my mother was simply another name on the guest list. I was pretty laid back about this party—we even waited until the baby was born to ascertain my need for baby clothes. Mostly, I just wanted to show the baby off. My sister was flying down to represent the family and I didn't really care if my mother made the hour and a half drive up. Or so I thought . . .

When the big day came, my mother called and asked if it mattered whether she came or not. She was tired and the drive was a pain and we'd seen her a lot in the past month. I said I didn't mind, and at that moment, I believed it. Then I hung up. Suddenly, I couldn't believe she didn't care enough to come to her own daughter's baby shower. I was devastated. I picked up the phone to call her back a dozen times, but pride made me hang up. Then I got angry. If she didn't want to be there, then it must not be important. What did it matter? Why should I care? Besides, I still had to shower and nurse the baby and put on mascara for the first time in weeks. I threw myself into the task. By the time I had my dress on, there was a knock on the door. She must have driven at the speed of light! I was so happy to see her I cried through my mascara and had to start all over again.

A baby shower is similar to a Christening or a Bris: it's a rite of passage for the new family. If your daughter-in-law is having the baby, it's even more important to participate. Since it may not be your natural inclination, it will mean a great deal more in the long run. And it really is the "long run" that you are investing in now. If you have the shower, it will forge a real relationship between the two of you. If someone else has the shower, your enthusiastic attendance will reflect your good intentions and help you become friends in the interest of the baby.

Some baby showers are thrown as couples parties— barbecues, brunches or even cocktail soirees. With the men in the family present, it may be even easier to participate. Take advantage of this opportunity. Be on the "welcome wagon" for your grandchild. Sharing these happy events will build a lasting bond with the expanding family.

How To Help During Labor

Your Daughter

If you are interested in being there during labor, discuss the possibilities with your daughter in advance. In all the excitement, she may not have thought about it. Assure her that you'll do whatever makes her feel the most comfortable. Let your desires be known, then follow hers.

If you are invited, go! Reminisce about your own delivery without making light of hers. Tell jokes, tell stories, tell the nurses to bring ice chips! Remember, any distraction is a good distraction.

If you can't be there, be in touch. Send flowers immediately. Mail her a copy of the New York Times or L.A. Times printed on the baby's birthday to save for posterity. Better yet, send a new bathrobe or casual outfit appropriate for the jubilant trek home from the hospital. By the end of nine months, most new mothers are as anxious for a change of clothes as they are to have that baby! When shopping, think cheerful, loose and easy access for breastfeeding.

Your Daughter-in-Law

If your presence has been requested and you feel comfortable about being there, go right ahead. Otherwise, wait to visit until after the baby is born. My friend's mother-in-law was allowed in the Labor & Delivery room by the friendly hospital staff. Vicky loves her mother-in-law, but she would have appreciated some privacy. If you recall, childbirth is a very messy ordeal. Vicky was a little embarrassed and felt she deserved more respect. More importantly, she wanted her husband all to herself. After so much effort, she needed some personal attention.

Your daughter-in-law doesn't want to make waves. So, it's up to you to test the water before you jump in. Once the baby is born, you can ingratiate yourself into the household best by making things as easy as possible for the parents. Cook dinner, hire a maid service, entertain the other children, or watch the baby so the parents can take a much needed nap. Follow their lead and they'll value you greater than gold.

If you cannot be there in person, call often. Keep the conversation brief. Send a gift that will stand out from the crowd: his and hers slippers (for nighttime feedings), a roll of film, a lullaby tape, a petit point baby announcement or a personalized baby blanket.

Your Baby's Baby

The greatest bond on Earth is between mother and child. There is no more touching picture than a woman with her newborn. A father rounds out the portrait nicely. However, most women say that even in this ideal circumstance, there is something missing from the picture. It is an emotional emptiness, a desire for their own mother to be there.

In fact, many new parents' biggest disappointment after childbirth is that their mothers aren't there to share the spectacle of new life and complete the circle. During the birth of my younger child, my mother was busy caring for my oldest. I knew she would have loved to be with me, yet I still felt that empty space.

If you can, be there for your baby. Be there for your baby's baby. Be there for you. Grandchildren are the second greatest bond.

Bonding

Do you believe in love at first sight? It's a common phenomenon with grandbabies. The first cry makes you appreciate the miracle of creation. The first look jump-starts your heart into a lifelong love affair. When I first mentioned "bonding" to my husband, he asked if it was anything like Bondo, the glue. I had to laugh . . . but, actually, it is. Once you're smitten, you're pretty well stuck. That's why seeing the baby is vital: visual imprinting makes a difference! The more time you spend with your grandchild early on, the closer you'll feel to the child as he or she grows up—even compared to your other grandchildren.

A word of warning before you rush to the hospital to hold the newborn: *beware of Mommy's possessiveness.* Breastfeeding guarantees a certain amount of intimacy, but that might not be enough. For some reason, I expected my mother to help out with the new baby by helping out with the house. You know, the laundry, the meals—the yucky stuff. After one load of laundry, she made her intentions clear. It was the baby she wanted and the baby she'd have. I had to bribe her to give me the baby back! We teased her and called her "the Grandma from Hell." She didn't care what we said as long as she got to hold the baby. The image of her moving the baby out of my reach makes me laugh even now. The fact is, neither of us had realized how much we wanted the baby to ourselves. So, be forewarned: wait your turn for the baby. Soon, the new mother will be only too happy let you soothe that baby indefinitely. "Okay, Mom, your turn now . . . please!"

If you are unable to meet the baby right away or to stay for any amount of time, there are many other ways to bond with your new grandchild. Put a big photograph of you (holding the baby, ideally) near the bassinet or the changing table. Babies love faces—yours will become familiar and welcome. Plastic Key rings are a popular infant toy, and at least one brand includes indestructible photo frames. It is the perfect gift for a teething infant and to help develop tactile skills. Recognizing your picture and those of others she loves will be a bonus. Address the olfactory senses by sending a scarf or comfort blanket with your scent. Wear it, sleep with it, add a dash of your perfume and the baby will know whenever you are near. Another fun way to bond is through sound. Send an audio tape of your favorite lullaby for the baby to listen to at bedtime; on the flip side, record nursery rhymes for playtime. Sing those tunes on the telephone and in person, and you'll be regarded as the special friend you are—Grandma.

The Name Game

What do you want to be called? Pick a name—any name—and stick with it. Many silly sounding nicknames are simplifications so the baby can say it easily—and earlier. Some are actually derivatives from other languages. Around the world, "grandma" sounds like this:

Ouma	Afrikaans
Sitt	Arabic
Baba	Bulgarian
Zu-mu	Chinese
Mormor	Danish
Oma'	Dutch
Grandmother	English
Grandma	
Grandnana	
Granny	
Nana	
Nanny	

Club Grandma

• • • • • • •

Aana Maurling	Eskimo
Isoäité Mummi	Finnish
Grandmère Grandmama	French
Grossmutter	German
Yiayia	Greek
Kupua wahine Tutu	Hawaiian
Savta	Hebrew
Nagyanana	Hungarian
Mama Seanmhathair	Irish
Nonna	Italian
Oba-San	Japanese
Hal Mo-ni	Korean
Mormor	Norwegian
Babeir	Polish
Avó	Portuguese
Buniea	Romanian
Babushka	Russian
Abuela Abuelita	Spanish

Nyanya	Swahili
Mormos	Swedish
Büyük anne	Turkish
Bà	Vietnamese
Mamqu Naim	Welsh
Bobe	Yiddish
Ukhula Isalukazi	Zulu

Any name will work. It doesn't matter what they call you . . . as long as they call you, right?

You know you're a member of Club Grandma when . . .

— the man of your dreams is six years old.
— your phone bill would pay off the national debt.
— you know the difference between Bert and Ernie.
— you immediately see a family resemblance in the squalling newborn's face.
— you send the children home.

3.

⊛ ⊛ ⊛ ⊛ ⊛ ⊛ ⊛

Member Benefits

*Spoil them, love them, indulge them, then send them
back to their parents to civilize them again.*
—Joan McIntosh, American writer

R aising children is as tough as it is rewarding. You will always be a mother. But, being a grandmother is a lot more fun. In fact it's both revenge and reward.

Yesterday, as I was being fitted for new reading glasses, I mentioned to the optometrist that I needed a sturdy frame to withstand the yanking of tiny little hands. It was like I'd opened the floodgate. The woman exclaimed, "Oh my goodness, I love being a Grandma! This weekend my granddaughter stayed at our house and slept with us. She kicked a lot, but I didn't care, it was so much fun, all that kissing and giggling. We gave her ice cream for dinner and let her stay up late."

"Sounds like fun," I said.

"I especially love not having to discipline her,." She added. "That's not my job,"

"Oh, Grandpa does that?" I asked.

"No, no, her parents do that. Our job is to spoil her and give her back. Best job I ever had," she declared.

All this, completely unbidden. I doubt I can write off my doctor's appointment in the name of research, but it goes to show you how universal this joyful act of grandparenting really is.

Here are some of the fun benefits for members of Club Grandma.

A Special Friendship

Forget rules and routines. Kids just want to have fun—and you're just the person to share it with. Your unique position in the family attracts natural adoration from the grandchildren. After all, you love them no matter what, no expectations or requirements. They've passed the test by being born. This is the ideal situation for becoming best friends and confidants. They can confide in you because they expect emotional support rather than rationality and behavior lessons.

My three-year-old granddaughter told her mother that she got a small burn on her hand because the window bit her. Obviously, she wished that were the truth. She admitted to me that her hand touched the toaster when she put the bread in. She knew her mother would have followed up my sympathy with a stern reminder that she was not to use the toaster by herself, nor to stand on a chair to reach it. I wasn't obligated to do anything but comfort the child. The lesson had already been learned.

As a grandma, you are a friend with special power. You are a friend who can make toast. Better yet, you are a friend who can reach the cookie jar!

The Material World

Juliette loves to primp for Nana. And I dare say, judging from some of the outfits my mother turns up in, she makes a special effort as well. It's fun to dress up for somebody who truly appreciates your essence. No need to throw away that Mickey Mouse watch—your grandchildren will love seeing it on you. Keep those wardrobe cast-offs for dress-up. Clothes and accessories have a new life with grandchildren.

The True You

Children don't care what you do in the real world. Oh sure, teenagers might be impressed that you're a Supreme Court Judge, but mostly they'll appreciate you for being yourself. You can relax and enjoy yourself with these people who love you mainly because you exist. You can drop the outside roles and pretenses. My daughter and mother enjoy pretending they are each other. Nana will be Juliette for a few hours, and vice versa. It gets confusing sometimes, but I know Juliette must love Nana a lot if she so enjoys being her.

If you value yourself, the children will value you as well. In turn, you'll value yourself more and realize, after all this time, who you truly are.

Freedom

Contrary to popular belief, close family relationships create independent individuals. The emotional support acts as a secure base from which you can leap into the world and fly. With this security, you'll find yourself more self-reliant, more active and more social than ever before. No longer are you defined by your work or marital status: you are a grandma, a well-loved and respected member of society. You are free to do whatever makes you happy.

Take the Good Time with You

Since you are not constantly in attendance, "photograph" the happy moments with your grandchildren in your mind. You can ignore negative situations by making the event good for you and creating a happy memory to remember it by. Let's say your birthday picnic was rained out, your son and his wife fought all day, and your granddaughter had a noisy tantrum. Recapture that exquisite moment when she helped you blow out the candles then hugged you with all her might. Later, take that picture out and enjoy those warm fuzzy feelings again. When someone asks how your birthday was, you can say it was wonderful.

V.I.P.

Everything you do is special, by definition. So, you can teach your way of doing things. Not bad things, just the usual things—but your way. A little power goes a long way. Setting the table, making the bed—there are many different methods for even ordinary tasks. You can let your grandchildren in on a special technique and chuckle when you hear them tell their parents they want to do it Grandma's way.

Keep in mind that fun with you encompasses a wide range of activities. Something described as a "chore" at home or "work" at school can be "fun" with you. Teaching your grandchild how to write thank-you notes falls well within the fun category as long as it is an activity shared with you. Grandma's smile is infectious.

The Sky's the Limit

Learn new skills without embarrassment. So you've never quite caught up to the computer age? No problem. Your grandchildren will be thrilled to teach you. They get to show off and be the experts—you get to learn without pressure. In return, you can visit the putting range together and teach them how to play golf.

Adult Relationships

Grandchildren will bring you and your child closer. Your children may be grown, but this is probably the first time you can truly enjoy an adult relationship with them. In the world of parenting, you are now peers. Once I became a mother, I definitely saw my own mother in a different light—one of respect and, yes, appreciation. I can still feel angry *with* her, but it's different. We can relate. We're friends. I actually call *her* now . . . for advice or just to chat.

You can see parts of your children in their children. And that's not all. . . .

Every time I look at the grandchildren, I see another relative. Of course, in each of them, I also see me. I figure, now their parents have to deal with me from both directions. I try to go easy on them.

Life

Grandparents live longer. Have you heard the statistics that show married men live longer than unmarried men, because they are loved and taken care of? Do you know a couple who passed away within weeks of each other? Human contact is vital to us all. We live for love.

My mother-in-law was ill when we met. My husband and I were married three years before our first child was born, but she hung in there. When Juliette was eight weeks old, we flew up to Seattle to introduce them. I'll never forget the joy on the new Grandma's face when she held that baby. What was she thinking of when she looked into Juliette's eyes? Immortality? Completing the circle of life? That night, Grandma Jean was put in the hospital and we spent the next day visiting her there. She held the baby and chuckled a lot. Her eyes were sparkling—she was strong and full of life. Weeks later, she passed away. She is with us always, not only in our hearts, but also in a photograph of our visit that hangs on the wall. Juliette loves to look at that picture.

If you think you've lived long enough in this world, hold on. Experience your grandchild. Let your grandchild experience you. It's worth the wait. Love is everything.

Spirituality

Now that you are connected with the future, doesn't every little thing seem related to one grand scheme of things? Whether or not you practice a formal religion, the existence of some higher power is likely to be in your thoughts. You have experienced the essence of nature itself.

Many grandparents initiate the habit of bedtime prayers. It can be the start of a spiritual bond between you and the forces that brought you together. No other time may seem as peaceful as when your grandchild says her prayers and you tuck her safely in bed. It establishes a special relationship between the two of you. Helping a child give thanks surely lays a sparkling path to Heaven.

You know you're a member of Club Grandma when . . .

— you don't mind being drooled on.
— you spend $60 on a velvet party dress that will be outgrown in three months.
— you hang up the phone and realize you forgot to talk to your son.
— you believe coloring on the walls demonstrates creativity.
— you get a special feeling that never goes away.

4.

◉ ◉ ◉ ◉ ◉ ◉

Tips for New Members

*The quickest way to be convinced that spanking is
unnecessary is to become a grandparent.*
—Anonymous

Here are some inside tips especially for new members of Club Grandma:

1. "Help" Is a Four-Letter Word

Beware of being invasive. Your unsolicited advice, helpful as it might be, could be considered meddlesome. This is tricky, because when your child calls you with a problem, it sounds like she is looking for a solution. Yet, that might not be the case. Unless she specifically asks for suggestions, it is safest to assume that she wants you to listen, acknowledge her feelings and be understanding.

Be careful even in simple situations: if you pitch in by making lunch for the kids, find out what their parents want them to eat. Mom and Dad know how you can be truly helpful. If you want to help, check with them first.

2. Get Out the Scrapbooks!

Now is your chance to coo over pictures of your son in his sailor suit. Children love to see their parents as youngsters.

They enjoy comparing their looks and behavior. It helps them understand growing up, lets them poke harmless fun at their parents and allows you both to have a great time.

3. "I Am Not Your Grandma"

The name that future generations call you is the emotional embodiment of your family relationship. It's personal. Nobody else needs to call you this name. My mother was dating a man who called her "Grams" once. She loves being a grandma—she doesn't hide it. After all, there is a crib in her living room. It is very possible that the man meant it with every bit of respect that was due. Nevertheless, it was their last date. Put an end to impersonal use of this title, except as a description of merit.

4. Fountain of Youth

Being a grandmother is the best excuse there is to be a kid again. They might guess that you're 100, but they have no concept of what that really means. To the contrary, they will naturally assume that you have the same preposterous amount of energy that they do!

Kids love to play games—any games. From peek-a-boo to charades, games keep everyone on their toes. (They also teach valuable skills and behavioral lessons.)

In poetry, youth is often described as the age of wonder. Shed your preconceptions and join your grandchildren in staring at the clouds. Explore every leaf and twig on a tour around the same old block. Get reacquainted with the child in you. Children make you young at heart.

31

5. Open House

Leave out your welcome mat and you'll always be welcome at your grandchildren's house. When the children feel comfortable in your environment, it's natural that they'll want you to share their turf. Public relations experts stress that participation equals belonging. Be part of the family. Help yourself to a glass of juice, and allow them to do the same at your house.

If you live close enough, this policy will keep you warm through the winter. Parents want to keep their children happy. If that means going to Grandma's house or inviting you over, make it easy for them. Always call before you want to drop in. Ask that they always check with you as well. Face it, sometimes we're just not up to seeing people, even those we love. Respect each other's privacy, and you'll enjoy more time together.

If you live far away, extend a blanket invitation to them, with the requirement of checking your schedule first. Ask when a good time to visit their house would be and stress that they needn't clear the decks to entertain you. To really get to know the children, join them in their regular activities. Take them to the park, watch a martial arts class or enjoy their reactions to the latest sing-along video. Bring your own entertainment—books, crocheting, movie money or walking shoes—to fill in the time. Offer to baby-sit so the parents can have dinner out. Beware, they may want to keep you!

6. Indispensable You

You are the best baby nurse, the best sitter, and the best party helper because you have a vested interest. In an emergency, would you rather they call a stranger? If your grandchild has a problem he is afraid to ask Mommy about, wouldn't it be nice if he called you? You can be the heroine in times of need.

Be a part of the family even when you live far away. Give the baby a toy phone to play with, then call up and speak with him over the real one. As a birthday present, give a cuddly doll for the child to remember you by. Soft animals made of parachute silk are a nighttime necessity at our house—and machine washable. Buy two copies of your favorite bedtime book and read in tandem over the phone on Sunday nights when the rates are low. Record yourself singing lullabies to soothe the baby to sleep. Become part of the day to day reality of your grandchildren. That way, they'll be a part of yours.

7. You Are Not Alone

Some of you are raising your grandchildren, perhaps by yourself. All of you can utilize the many support systems that have sprung up to enrich the special relationship between you and your grandchild. Local organizations are available to help. Look to the elementary school system, adult education programs at the community college, plus area churches and synagogues for special programs aimed at you. Many "Mommy & Me" classes offered at hospitals and birthing programs welcome grandmothers with open arms. Informal play groups can be formed through word of mouth or a friendly pediatrician. Private support groups are springing up under the domain of family therapists. My mother's therapy group for menopausal women routinely deals with the joys and challenges of being a grandparent.

On the lighter side, Gymboree and other commercial activity classes for children are seeing a growing number of grandparents involved in the programs. Organizations like the Young Grandparents Club (where young is a state of mind) are listed in national parenting magazines and are forming groups nationwide. If your town has a local parents newspaper, read it. In fact, read everything you can find. The other day, I noticed a column for grandparents in a union newsletter. Other grandmothers are out there—take a stroll to the neighborhood park and you'll see. Practice pick-up lines like "How many grandchildren do you have?" and "How old is the baby?" You are not alone. In fact, you'll never be alone again!

8. Assertiveness Training

"I love you but the answer is no" works for grandparents as well as parents. You know how to deal with the little ones. It's the big ones that get out of hand. Tell them "no," you can't baby-sit next weekend, you've already made plans. Be honest when you just want that time for yourself. That way, you'll never resent the time that you do spend with them.

My mother is very specific about her schedule. When we are together, I know that she's happy about it. It makes life easier than reading between the lines. In return, when she wants to stay over an extra night, I can tell her I'd rather have some family time alone. Often, we bring the children down to her house with a real date in mind. Generally, this backfires . . . once we're there, my husband would rather just stay home and relax while Nana deals with the children. Plus, he likes my mother.

If you don't feel like listening to your daughter's problems right now, tell her. You'll be more help when you *are* in the mood. The first time I called my mother in the middle of "Barbara Walters," she said she'd call me back, then hung up on me. I admit, it was a bit upsetting. Now, I realize this practice saves me from repeating myself when she's not paying attention. Plus, I can watch my tape of "All My Children" in peace. Encourage your children to be honest about sharing their time. When you can say "no," "yes" becomes a joy for everyone.

9. Sleeping Beauty

My favorite part about spending the weekend with my mother is sleeping in. For parents of young children, that means eight o'clock, at least! Those precious extra hours of rest guarantee that I'll be loving, kind and incredibly grateful for the rest of the day. For my mother, it means starting her day with the people who most adore her in the world. Most children are at their best in the morning: happy and raring to go. Nana enjoys this time with the children more than any other . . . thank goodness! You will, too.

Baby Catherine has a solar sensitive cell—if the sun is up, so is she. Her parents have tried everything, from putting her to bed late to blocking out the windows—nothing works. I know she didn't get this from me. I was never much of an early riser. In self-defense, I made up a game with the baby. Once she was awake and making sounds, I'd go stand by the crib. I put out my arms and repeated my name over and over, but I wouldn't pick her up until she said it. Something that sounded like it, anyway. Okay, I didn't refuse her when she got frustrated the first few times, but she was a quick study. Now, I tease her to call my name then I sweep her out of the crib. I love to hear her call "Nana." I take it personally. So, despite the early hour, I start the day with a thrill.

35

Feeding and dressing children are easy activities, plus you can probably get away with watching "Sesame Street" or "Bugs Bunny." If this effort wears you out, nap with the younger ones later on. Your grandchildren won't always be little. Besides, there's always tomorrow to catch those extra forty winks!

10. Routine Fun

Wouldn't it be nice to know when you'll see your grandchildren again? Even if you live close by, it can be difficult to see the children regularly. Life gets in the way. The solution is to add yourself to their calendar. If you see each other every month, you can create a tradition of taking the child to lunch or for a stroll or to the library or to the petting zoo. Perhaps you could finish off with a bath and a bedtime story.

If you would like to see them more often, become a part of the permanent schedule. You could take the baby to a weekly "Baby and Me" class. You could be the chauffeur for the older child's dance classes or swimming lessons. You could host dinner or baby-sit every Thursday. You could assign one morning a week to the preschoolers and plan crafts projects or field trips. The possibilities are endless. Decide what you would enjoy doing the most, then find out what works best for everyone.

11. Create Occasions from Afar

The best advice for all members of Club Grandma is to insinuate yourself into the day-to-day life of your grandchildren. It's easy to do, even if you live 3,000 miles away. Simply build ordinary days into exciting events.

Club Grandma

• • • • • •

The first day of school is always a big deal, but you can make it into a momentous event in your relationship.

I spoke with Juliette about her first day of nursery school for several weeks before hand. We counted down to it, marked days off the calendar and played make-believe school with Juliette as the teacher. I sent her a good luck card in the mail, then called her the night before to share her anticipation and ease her concern. I called after school to see how it went. Now, when Juliette remembers going to school, I know she thinks of me as part of it.

Be careful about putting pressure on children with your expectations of performing well for the occasion. Just encourage a happy experience. Don't highlight events that are too far away for the child to relate to. Celebrating a half-birthday or the birthday of the family pet or even the start of hockey season can bring you closer to an older child.

Create an occasion out of thin air by setting a date during your next visit to watch soccer practice or to see a new movie. Any occasion with you will be a special one.

You know you're a member of Club Grandma when . . .

— you spend an entire day with your daughter-in-law.
— the baby cries in the middle of the night and you don't have to get up.
— you hear "Grandma" and realize someone's talking to you.
— animal crackers are a staple of your grocery list.

5.
⦾ ⦾ ⦾ ⦾ ⦾ ⦾ ⦾

Active Members

Age doesn't protect you from love.
But love, to some extent, does protect you from age.
—Jeanne Moreau

Your Many-Splendored Roles

Grandmas are more than just fun and games. The children may not know this, but it's true. Your importance cannot be overstated. In fact, many traditional grandmother activities have been taken over by surrogates since the demise of the extended family. Fast-food serves as home cooking, family therapists help with family problems, celebrities are heroes, television offers stereotypes of aging, and movies provide a sense of history. Unfortunately, these surrogates aren't madly in love with the children like you are. Active members of Club Grandma do all these things—much better.

1. Influence

Your influence is overwhelming. You may think everything you say goes in and one ear and out the other, but the strangest thing happens in the middle. Those words are burned into memory! Be gentle. In regular discussions with the children, be careful that your influence is positive.

When Juliette was struggling with potty training, Nana was the only one who could get away with teasing her. One day, Juliette missed the potty entirely. I tried not to be angry about the mess, but I was disappointed. Nana just laughed. She didn't shame Juliette by calling her a baby, insult her by saying she was bad nor discourage her by emphasizing the error. Instead, she trickled Juliette and showed her a better way to try it next time. She reinforced the positive: it was an honest effort.

In private, I suggested that the parents throw away the stickers and gummy bears and everything else they were using to lure Juliette to the potty. I said Juliette would use the potty when she was ready. Secretly, I wasn't sure when she'd be ready . . .

Nana hadn't said much of anything up until this point, so when she spoke, I listened. She was right. It wasn't until Juliette realized that she was a big girl, on her third birthday, that she truly paid attention to nature's call.

When it comes to advice, less is more.

2. Respect

Who are the most powerful people in a child's universe? Parents. Daddy typically means playtime: Mommy means business. She is the boss. You are not the boss. You are a far superior being: the boss's boss. When my mother reminds my daughter that I was in her tummy long ago, that little girl's eyes grow wide. It helps her to understand that older people are individuals worthy of respect.

Respect works both ways: don't forget to treat the children with respect. Acknowledge a child's feelings whether or not they are justified. A child is especially vulnerable. He cannot help what he feels. Once you let him know you understand that he is angry or sad, then you can address his behavior. In turn, he will learn to respect your feelings.

Teenagers learn to respect the elderly from you, no matter how old you are. Don't be insulted; letting go of cultural stereotypes is always good. Teenagers are rarely treated as important people by adults, so be sure to let them know you respect them. Relate to each as an individual. Soon, you'll have a friendship at the deepest level. You'll each blossom and know a special person cares.

3. Protector

Who can protect those precious children from the cold, cruel world? You. Kids know they can count on Grandma. It can be simple, like when you insist on a nap. You are actually protecting them from fatigue. Or, it can be complicated, like when World War III erupts in their own home. Then, you can comfort them over the telephone, remove them temporarily from the situation and be there for emotional support.

When you are with your grandchildren, you unconsciously protect them from strangers as well as hurt feelings. If they're embarrassed to tell Daddy about the school-yard bully, you can take the matter into your own capable hands—it's fun to go to the rescue.

> When Juliette was twenty months old, I took her to the park near her house. A four-year-old girl grabbed Juliette's shovel and refused to give it back. Juliette immediately looked over to the bench where I was sitting and cried out, "Nan!".

Needless to say, the prodigal child got her shovel back in a jiffy. Both she and Nana were very pleased about the whole incident. Super Grandma to the rescue!

4. Teacher

You don't need a degree in Early Childhood Education to be a great teacher to your grandchild. Everything you do serves as an example of good conduct. This starts with the basics. As a baby, your grandchild will copy the sound you make when you click your tongue. Try it! She'll blow kisses after seeing you blow them to her. She'll learn to talk by repeating words that you say.

Later on, things get a little more complicated. She will continue to learn by mimicking behavior—not just her parents' actions, but yours as well. She will unconsciously begin to think along the same lines. Ethics and values are the most vital elements of a person's behavior throughout their life. These lessons are learned early and you are an excellent source for them. Be good!

On a more literal level, you are also the best history teacher they'll ever have, Ivy League or not. Children love stories. Tales of your experience in the real world teach them about that world in a direct, non-threatening manner. My grandfather was a young child when his family escaped from Russia in 1917. Visions of the family jewels sewn into his jacket as his sled was pulled over the snow during that midnight escape make the Bolshevik Revolution come alive for me. My great-grandfather's promotion of Gypsy Rose Lee, as told by my late maternal grandmother, have made the vaudeville era a reality as well. Describe your life in terms of the big picture. It's more glamorous than you might think. Mostly, it just needs details to make it personal. Did you collect tin cans after World War II? Nana remembers stepping on them. Did you wear love beads during the sixties? Nana wore a medallion that read "War is unhealthy for children and other living things." School history books are not only boring to children forced to read them, but they are also surprisingly inaccurate. Their content relies a great deal on current political trends. For example, the Vietnam War wasn't mentioned in most history books until over a decade later. And it hasn't been long since Native Americans were portrayed only as bad guys. Make history come alive for your grandchildren. Teach them well.

5. Role Model

For Granddaughters

To your granddaughter, you are the prime example of what a mature woman should be. Of course, she gets the basics from her mother. That relationship, however, is fraught with other concerns. At times, she will be prone to rebel from her mother's shadow. You are the distinct archetype. Help her standards be high.

For Grandsons

Have you ever heard the claim that the way a man treats his mother is a precursor of the way he'll treat his wife? Let's take this theory a little farther: if your grandson respects and values you he is likely to do the same with other mature woman. Your part is simply to be a good role model, so give him something to work with. When you hear how he helped a woman pick up the groceries that fell out of her bag, give yourself a pat on the back.

6. Caregiver

Forget daycare, television and baby-sitters: you are the real thing. If you are able to offer any time to your grandchildren, be assertive about it. Even if it is convenient and you are willing, your children may not want to trouble you. They consider this to be a job, and justifiably so.

My mother dreams of the day when my girls can walk to her house after school on a warm afternoon for milk and cookies. In the real world she has to work, we live too far away and I'm not sure if she even knows how to bake cookies! My husband dreams of a ranch with the Grandmother House on the property. For now, we compromise with emergency situations, lots of telephone time and an afternoon at least one weekend a month. If you live across the country, talk to your grandchildren about what they watch on television. Ask about their daycare activities. Visit the nursery school when you are in town.

Where did this term "caregiver" come from, anyway? My guess is that it's a politically correct combination of caretaker, nanny, helper, friend, housekeeper, babysitter, surrogate Mommy . . . in short: Grandma! You can be your child's favorite caregiver.

The Key: Keep in Touch

Keeping in touch is the key to how active members of Club Grandma stay active. Here are some fun ways to do it, no matter where you live:

1. Make Plans for Every Holiday!

Celebrate together—not necessarily in person. Did you ever linger at the greeting card store and wander into strange and unusual categories? Now you know someone who will dearly love to receive a card with a jack-o-lantern on it! Here is your chance to carve a pumpkin again, even if you live alone. Be sure to send a photograph of your creation so you can all enjoy it.

Be part of the fun at Easter by dyeing eggs with your grandchildren. If you can't be together, do some anyway and describe how you decorated your eggs in an Easter card. Some gift stores celebrate the season by dressing someone up in a rabbit costume and offering free Polaroids for the children. During Hanukah, send them chocolate gelt and ask their parents to give them each a "coin" from you after lighting the candles each night. At Christmas, go to the mall and get your picture taken with Santa. Why not? Just tell Santa's helpers that you're a child at heart, then send the photo to your grandchildren.

Start celebrating your birthday again. Have them count down with you—it will reinforce the fact that you are special enough for birthdays, too. Make a birthday cake and tell them all about it. Ask them to make you a card by hand. This could even be an excuse for a visit. If your children are dubious, tell them that in Hawaiian families, all the relatives gather on Grandma's birthday for a party that lasts for days!

It's funny how we go through phases of celebrating holidays. When you are little, you count down to them with glee. Holidays are what separates the days from, well, all the other days. When you are dating, holidays are an excuse for social events. When you are married, they become a new ritual. Not long after that, you get busy and skip them altogether. Then, you have children and start all over again. By the time you have grandchildren, you understand that rituals are important. You know how to celebrate, too!

2. Call Them!

Just say good morning or good night—without talking to the folks. Your grandchildren will feel important to get a person-to-person phone call. Having someone who loves them at the other end of the line is an extra bonus. That will be one special phone call! Rest assured, the call can be short (meaning inexpensive). After all, you don't need to discuss world peace . . . and if you do, what better audience?

Even infants like to hear your voice. Don't be hurt if they're not in the mood to have the phone laid to their ear. There's always tomorrow, when they might actually "talk" to you. There's no dictionary for babyspeak, so just assume they're saying "I love you" and take it from there.

Nana is convinced that babies say "I love you" with that very first babble. For a more intelligible version, you could encourage them to watch "Barney," the TV show with the friendly purple dinosaur. The theme song begins "I love you, you love me, we're a happy family . . ." sung to the tune of "This Old Man." Catherine, my one-year-old, sings what sounds convincingly like "I love you" nearly 24 hours a day. Yes, even on the telephone. I'm not sure she knows what she's saying, but I admit, I love it. My mother says there's no question that Catherine knows what she is saying. It's not clear, however, whether that's her "expert" opinion or her "Nana" opinion.

In any case, if you let your grandchildren know that you

love them, it won't be long until they really are saying "I love you."

3. Write Letters!

Whether you are down the block or across the country, it takes only a stamp to show you care. A letter can be many things, from a short note on a shopping list to a postcard of a frog. Once, Nana cut a heart from blank deposit slip and mailed that. Juliette got the message. For that matter, Nana once sent me an anonymous postcard with nothing but my address on it. The picture showed a woman trapped in a highchair by a giant-sized baby. I got the message, too. Of course, I recognized her perfect penmanship.

> I admit I keep the mailman busy. I clip things from the paper that might interest my grandchildren or their parents. I got the idea when I was a little girl spending the summer away at camp in Maine. My bunkmate's Grandma sent her articles and pictures and comics in the mail. I was jealous. I decided to be that kind of Grandma when I grew up.

If your grandchildren can't read yet, receiving mail will make them feel important. They will love being read a message that is especially for them. Once they memorize the contents (quicker than you might think), they will pretend to read it to themselves. Preschoolers will enjoy recognizing some of letters of the alphabet and will be motivated to learn to read. For elementary-age children, not only will getting the letter be fun, but reading it will also be good practice.

If you'd like to write, but aren't sure what to say, mention times that you shared recently or activities coming up. It's like courting—talk about them a lot and include yourself whenever you can!

4. Remember Friends

Write down the names of your grandchild's friends, just like you write spouse names in your address book for holiday cards. Ask about the friends by name. Even if, as with many children, their friends change weekly, there will be at least one name that is consistent. The child will appreciate that you cared enough to try. Think how pleased you'd be if your grandchildren asked about *your* friends!

5. Learn Your Grandchild's Schedule

Remember what day dance class falls on. Then, when you call, write or see them in person, you can ask about how their day went. My daughter is one of those children who will answer "fine" until the cows come home. Nana solves this dilemma by asking her about specific activities with one vital detail glaringly wrong. She'll ask what Juliette did at Casey's house when, in fact, she knows very well that Juliette had been at Tara's home. Juliette will boil over with frustration and not only straighten Nana out as to whose home she played at, but what activity they did there that they don't do at the other place. Sometimes it's most clever to act like you're not so clever.

6. Emphasize Things in Common

I used to think my mother was crazy when suddenly, and for no apparent reason, she'd smile at Juliette and blurt out that both she and Juliette loved chocolate ice cream. Now, for one thing, who doesn't like chocolate ice cream? For another thing, why tell me now? Finally, why tell me at all? At dinner, when Juliette wasn't hungry, Nana would talk about how she and Juliette both hate spinach. At the pool, she'd point out that she had green in her bathing suit, and Juliette had green in her hat. While helping with bath time, Nana would say that she has soft skin on her shoulders just like Juliette . . . then they would take turns feeling how soft they were. They were driving me nuts!

Finally it dawned on me. Every time my mother mentioned something—anything—that she and her granddaughter had in common, Juliette smiled. Whether it was that they both hate sand in their shoes, they both like bubble gum, or they both love getting mail, it made no difference. The more, the better. Juliette loves having things in common with her Nana. Now, SHE points out things they have in common. Perhaps this game helps develop cognitive thinking. The important part is that the game makes them feel close; the best part is that it's easy. Try it, you'll see.

7. Send Teeny-tiny Momentos

Kids love getting surprises. Stickers, a headband or colored shoelaces are tangible proof that you care. My three year-old insists that presents are wrapped; surprises are not. Even a box of raisins can be a good surprise—almost anything unexpected is a treat.

If you are a frequent visitor, don't bring gifts every time. They should look forward to you, not the gift. After all, you are the best gift they'll ever have. If you have more spending money than the parents, help where it counts, with diapers or dancing class.

If you still can't resist, once in a while treat the parents to some unexpected goodie like fresh bagels or real maple syrup. They need attention, too.

8. Share Your Favorite Childhood Book

Be forever connected to that story in their mind. Don't let them keep it with their other books. It should have a special place to live—so it has a special place in their heart.

9. Teach Your Favorite Song

Kids are no music critics, they won't care what you sound like. They will, however, remember the song. They'll feel close to you when they sing it, no matter where you are. If they happen to hear the song somewhere else, you can be sure they'll be thinking of you.

10. Get Personal with Gifts

Give gifts the children want—not just what you want them to have. Every year, Juliette receives a beautiful dress for her birthday from her great Grandma and great Grandpa. This year, they asked what else she liked and I mentioned her infatuation with Barney, the purple dinosaur. Her birthday turned into a Barney bonanza and she was the happiest little girl in America. Generally shy with relatives she doesn't see often, she couldn't wait to talk to Great Grandma and Grandpa on the phone. They took an active role in her life and she won't soon forget it. Oh, they also sent a beautiful dress!

If your grandchild longs for something you disapprove of, ask for another suggestion. Just remember, the more personal you get, the more personable your grandchild will be. Making a wish come true is a signal that you know them well. They will want to know you better.

Don't insist that your grandchild share her gift right away. Would you share your new cashmere sweater before you wore it? The child may be too young to have progressed through the "mine," "yours," "ours" phases of early childhood. You can encourage them to share some toys, but it's okay to have some special ones.

Give gifts with no strings attached. Don't expect anything in return. Feel free to ask about the gift when you speak with your grandchild. If they loved it, they may attach those emotions to you. But it's not a bribe. Try not to be disappointed if they exchange it for something else or give it to their best friend. Your goal is to make them happy.

You know you're a member of Club Grandma when . . .

— your idea of a good time includes microwave popcorn and a video of animals that sing.

— you stop worrying about what people will think.

— you believe that ice cream is in the dairy category of healthy food groups.

— your children no longer clean up before you visit.

6.

⬤ ⬤ ⬤ ⬤ ⬤ ⬤ ⬤

Official Duties

Do and you shall be.
—Camus

Be and you shall do.
—Sartre

Do be do be do.
—Sinatra

Never before have responsibilities been so pleasurable! As a member of Club Grandma, your official duties are divided among your grandchildren, your children and your self. Of course, the most vital concern for all of you is safety. Classes in Infant & Child CPR and Emergency First Aid are available through your local Red Cross chapter as well as many hospitals and YMCA's. Libraries and video stores often rent these tapes free as a public service. Once you have this safe foundation, you will be free to focus on the fun part—the relationships.

For the Grandchildren

1. Sense of Self

Have you ever been at a cocktail party where the woman next to you said, "Hi, nice party. So, what do you do?" Or, even worse, "Hi, nice party. So, what does your husband do?" Then, based on your answer, you watched the wheels turn in her head until something clicked and she decided you were worth talking to, or you weren't, and excused herself to put more dip on her cracker.

Now, pretend you are five years old. A girl with a shovel comes over to you at the park and says she'll play with you if you can build a sand castle. You want to play, but you're not quite sure if you can build a sand castle. It's enough to dissuade you from ever trying to build one.

Be proud of your grandson's batting average or school grades. But love him no matter what. Let the children know you value them for who they are, not what they are capable of doing. Next time you are at a party and someone asks what you do, reply that mostly, you enjoy talking to people who don't ask you that question. Then walk away. Find a telephone, call your grandson and tell him you love him—before he gets a chance to brag about his home run.

My mother has a sign in her home that reads: "I'm proud of what you've done but even more with what you are."

2. Unconditional Love

This should be listed as an FDA nutritional requirement for children. Telling them you'll love them more if they clean up their mess on your carpet is called performance based affection. This is the reward system. It is also called bribery. Do they have to bribe you for your love? Do you bribe them to love you with toys and treats? No, those things are extra. Your grandchildren love you for just being you.

Hear this! When a child seems the least lovable, that's the time when he needs your love most. Give him a hug. Be loving, in good times and bad. You can be a rock of emotional support in the stormy sea of childhood.

Do you feel lovable? In therapy, this simple question is the icebreaker for many couples in search of a closer relationship. You and your grandchild make a couple. Be lovable and you will be loved forever.

3. Comfort Zone

Hooray, Club Grandma means no more endless battles with kids! Now the little ones can run from mean old Mommy to you. You can be the softy. Not exactly good cop/bad cop, but an all around comfort zone—an escape from the day to day realities of discipline and growing up. In fact, you may find your defenses crumbling the moment your grandchildren are born.

As a grandmother, I've changed. It really hurts to hear my babies cry. If their parents feel the child should be allowed to cry, whether it's to soothe themselves to sleep or over a snack desired too close to dinnertime, I want to pick them up right away and comfort them. Even at the market, I'm tempted to pick up strangers' babies when they cry and the parents don't respond. I used to be tough. Now, I'm a cream puff.

As long as you are not interfering or undermining the parent's discipline, feel free to comfort your grandchildren at any time. They'll understand that the situation has not changed, but Grandma can make them feel better about it.

4. Validation

You can give the Grandma Stamp of Approval to everything good your grandchild does. Everyday battles over putting toys away can evolve into proud accomplishments when you validate the behavior. Pleasing you is special. With you to brag to, those tough tasks will not seem so hard after all.

Even other children will seek your validation. Grandma Sue attends every holiday party at her granddaughter's pre-school. When she missed St. Patrick's Day, the other children missed her. "Where's Grandma Sue?" It might be a party without you, but it won't be the same.

5. Tolerance

When you've seen it all before, it takes a lot to raise your eyebrows. Your grandson's imaginary dinosaur isn't so alarming when you think back to your daughter's invisible friend. It probably concerned you then the same way your grandson's behavior concerns your daughter now. Offer this tolerance to your grandson and your daughter will be able to relax as well. Many disturbing trends crop up throughout the different stages of growing up. Your grandchild will benefit from your relaxed attitude. After all, things that are "no big deal" generally don't last long enough to be harmful.

Remember the old adage that the strictest parents were the wildest ones in their youth? Here is your chance to savor your child's comeuppance. As a grandma, you can just smile like the Cheshire Cat, say nothing and feel saintly. Tolerance is a learned behavior—and a gift for others, as well.

6. Time

Oh, where do the hours go? Your children are rushing between work and family and—if they're lucky—friends. The phone, the fax, the groceries, the jobs . . . the only thing that doesn't stop is the clock. No wonder divorce is so prevalent—there's rarely time for the relationship. Most parents dream of leisurely picnics in the park with the kids. Didn't you? Now is your chance. Being a grandma means you get to savor the time you have to "hang out" with your grandchildren. You can have real conversations about the cosmos and their place in it. The more you know them, the better you'll like them. Your grandchildren will appreciate it, and you, all the more. Sounds cliché, but then, where do cliché's come from? The truth. Give the gift of time.

For Your Children

1. Emotional Support

Parenting has always been a difficult task. It is especially tough today when parents must guard their children from the life and death hazards of both public play and private indiscretions. We need someone to talk to. Who can we call when the baby cries all night? Who can we confer with when it is time to discuss AIDS and birth control? On the other hand, who will rejoice wish us when the baby first sleeps through the night? Or when the teenager turns down a drink and tells you about it? Who will understand—and care? Encourage your children to turn to you, in good times and bad. They need you.

2. Authority

Once you have the mother or father on the phone, ask if you can make a suggestion. As a parent, you've been there, so you are the best one to give advice. This does *not* mean your children must follow your advice. In desperate times, the parents can cite you directly as the authority, for example, "Grandma says it's important to use your manners." Never contradict or insult the parents in front of your grandchildren. It will only confuse and hurt them. By now, the little ones automatically believe what you say. Eventually, their parents will, too!

3. Pressure Valve

When your children are on overload, you can be a lifesaver. When the laundry is piled high, bills are stacking up and dinner is boiling over, you can pick up the fussy infant, offer a toy to the crying toddler and lovingly tease the sarcastic teenager. You can take them all outside for a bubble blowing contest or a short hike. Your children may need to deal with just one child for a few minutes. They may need to get dinner on the table. They may just need some time to relax. So, put on your sunblock and safety whistle. Grandma's here to save the day!

If you are far away, you can be just as much help as a sounding board. Get an answering machine (you need one now) with a speaker phone built in. This way, whenever your daughter needs to let off some heat, or your son had a bad day at the office, they can vent to you while you peruse your favorite magazine. Remember to say "my goodness " a lot!

Sometimes, I'm too embarrassed to talk to a friend and I'm too grumpy to unfairly harass my husband, so I'll call my mother. She'll turn down the news and help put things in perspective, or get me thinking about something completely different. For instance, once I've spilled my guts, it's wonderfully distracting to discuss her next opportunity to have the kids all to herself. Sometimes, Mom tells me about a resort she'd like to visit and we plan imaginary vacations. We even determine how warm it is, how the wind feels on our faces and how soft the lounge chairs are. Now that I think about it, this is a thinly veiled attempt of my mother's to use Guided Imagery to help me relax. It doesn't take a professional, just a caring grandma like you.

4. Negotiator

As the family matriarch (or Supreme One, as we say), you naturally have everyone's best interests in mind. So, when a fierce battle is raging, you are the ideal person to arbitrate. Even with conflicts over one-sided parental demands—like choosing a bedtime story, completing chores or going to bed—you can be a big help. If your youngest grandchild is screaming to stay up later, negotiate for a nap the next day. If she doesn't want naps at all, bargain for an earlier bedtime. With younger children, you can make a compromise feel like a victory.

If your relationship is good with your child's mate, you can help them, as well. Be fair, but don't go overboard. When asked, you can help from behind the scenes by offering your child some positive ways to work out the situation.

I used to show a film to my Family Development students at Ohio State. It showed a couple resolving conflict in three ways: accommodation—giving in; compromise—each getting something less than they want; and taking turns—my favorite. One common characteristic of dysfunctional families is that they never resolve the argument, they just move on. Whether the conflict is with your child and your grandchild or your child and their spouse, invite them to state their feelings, then think of ways to solve the problem. Ask them what's more important, being right or having a relationship?

At my house, the biggest fights have to do with who's making dinner. In other words, I don't want to. Hey, this is the nineties! With children, of course, somebody has to. My mother suggested writing down a schedule for which nights I had to cook, and which nights I didn't have to. My husband agreed, content that he could truly count on some hot meals without the side dish of resentment. I cook about the same amount now, but it's a lot more fun knowing I don't have to. Plus, I figure I get brownie points this way. (I'm saving up for some special occasion.) Schedules work for chores as well as things like who's turn it is to pick out the rental video. Even if the schedule is not adhered to, the air has been cleared and everyone realizes the value of cooperation.

5. Heroine

When I demonstrated a cartwheel for my three-year-old and cut my foot on the hammock, life at our house turned upside down. For a week, I was on crutches, unable to put an ounce of weight on my stitched-up foot. That translates into not being able to carry anything, from a glass of water to my nursing baby. After several days of juggling baby-sitters, camping out on my bed eating delivered pizza and whatever else my daughter could drag in from the kitchen, it was finally the weekend. My husband fumigated the house, made breakfast, then fainted at the pile of laundry. To give him a little credit, he did have his hands full between me and the kids. After all, he isn't a *mother!* Thank God for Nana. When her work week was over, she drove up with a homemade lasagna and did about eight loads of laundry. Then she went home for a golf date. My mother, my hero.

You are the best one to call in an emergency. You know

where everything is . . . and you care. Even if you can't be there physically, you can still help solve the problem.

6. Friend

It's true. Finally, you can be friends. You may not want to share the intimate details of your sex life, but certainly, you can chat about your favorite gown at the Academy Awards. When your focal length extends past your child to your grandchild, all that parental grief loosens up and, if you let it, dissolves into thin air—at least enough to start a new, improved relationship. Your child's emotional baggage, the myriad wrongs you supposedly committed, are no longer in the foreground. Be friends.

For You

Understanding The Children

How many times have you heard someone tell you their child's behavior is "just a phase" he is going through? Go ahead, roll your eyes. Most times, however, it *is* just a phase. The trick is to know which phase it is, what it means, and whether it should be encouraged or simply endured. After all, it is easier to love children—and adults—when you understand them.

Here is a simplified version of the socio-emotional developmental stages defined by renowned child development expert, Erik Erikson. Each stage of development offers a "critical period," a time when a certain skill must be achieved in order to lay the groundwork for future success.

Keep in mind that each child must learn at his own rate. The toddler who seems slow to toddle may be a large baby with extra weight to carry as he walks. He may be busy observing and thinking, in other words, learning. Children develop at different speeds, but in the same general progression.

It is important to note that failure to accomplish the goals of each stage can have far reaching effects well beyond childhood.

0–18 Months: Building Trust

The initial stage of life is "existence," which obviously takes a lot of adjustment. It is amazing how quickly a baby advances during the first year. An infant's primary behavior is reaching, usually for the caregivers (bonding).

Goal: emotional security.

Challenge: A baby is hungry and cries. His crying stops when he sees Mother or hears her footsteps, because he trusts he'll be fed. Mistrust comes from prolonged discomfort and anxiety—waiting too long for needs to be met.

Grandma's Role: To love, nurture and be consistent.

Appropriate Gifts: Soft, cuddly security blankets or dolls, textured and colorful items to explore the senses, and large, soft balls to encourage eye/hand coordination.

18 Months–3 Years: Building Autonomy

Becoming an individual means demonstrating power by doing "by myself": walking, climbing, grasping and letting go. The child also learns to control bodily functions. Self pride leads to strutting, talking and enjoying jokes.

Goal: Feelings of self worth lead to healthy curiosity and awe for life.

Challenge: If shamed by others he'll doubt himself, feel worthless and give up curiosity about the world.

Grandma's Role: Praise him. Offer choices to show you respect his opinion. Watch him practice new behavior, like stacking objects.

Appropriate Gifts: Blocks, pegboards and finger paints for developing motor skills, plus character figurines, trucks and tea sets for imaginative play.

4–5 Years: Initiative

As children move from attachment to exploration, they question and seek experience with purpose. Dramatic play teaches about life. When children feel guilty, they often repeat their parents' voices, telling them what they may or may not do. By now, they have developed a conscience. Too much control makes them fearful.

Goal: Curiosity leads to healthy exploration of the outside world, helping to create an understanding of the child's place within the world.

Challenge: If the children are taught that the swimming pool is dangerous, they may develop a fear of water. If they are taught the "safety rule" of staying away from the pool unless a grown-up is watching, then they will be free to explore water play when it is appropriate.

Grandma's Role: Talk with them, play with them and encourage their small steps towards independence.

Appropriate Gifts: Learning toys—clay, puzzles, books,

plus dramatic play items, including dress-up, kitchen sets, train sets.

6 to Puberty: Industry

These children want to do things! They are learning what they are capable of: dressing themselves, completing schoolwork, painting, dancing, playing sports, etc.

Goal: Achievement builds confidence.

Challenge: A child who does not feel confident in his abilities will soon feel inferior in all respects. This unworthiness will create a cycle of non-participation which eliminates further opportunity for achievement. This leads to a sense of inferiority.

Grandma's Role: Applaud their accomplishments. Go to the park and to their ball games. When a child is unsuited to a particular skill, encourage participation in alternative activities where another opportunity for success exists.

Appropriate Gifts: Items tailored to individual interests and hobbies.

Adolescence: Identity

Teenagers need to feel good about their sexually developing bodies. Feeling comfortable with themselves allows them to turn outward and care about things other than themselves. They struggle to find new values and beliefs, while rejecting those that don't fit. Healthy children learn to sympathize with other people. They develop genuine concern and commitment to the world around them.

Goal: To love themselves and know what they stand for.

Challenge: Teens with a poor sense of themselves search for belonging and can easily be led astray.

Grandma's Role: Show consistent interest in them as they try on new identities despite the outrageous clothing and hairstyles this search might involve.

Appropriate Gifts: Personalized items, trendy clothing, a session with a career counselor, a visit to a college of interest, leisurely walks . . . time alone with you.

Young Adulthood: Intimacy

Love is the dramatic interest of this age group. Each of the previous stages have laid the groundwork: trust, autonomy, initiative, industry and identity. Young adults can now be truly close to another human being in an intimate, committed relationship.

Goal: The ability to be ethically and emotionally intimate with another.

Challenge: Young adults need to allow themselves to be accepted and understood or they risk remaining isolated all their lives.

Grandma's Role: Be genuine and provide a shoulder to cry on. Be consistently loving and non-judgmental as they struggle with major life decisions.

Appropriate Gifts: Tickets for two for concerts, theatre or sports events; gift certificates for bookstores and music stores.

As you can see, your role is essentially the same throughout your grandchild's life: to love, nurture and be consistent.

Understanding Yourself

While babies develop, so do the rest of us. Parents, children and grandparents go through different stages of the life cycle at the same time. Open yourself up to the exploration of *you*. Grandmas are just as important as their grandchildren. Recognizing where you are coming from and where you are going will help you lead the children in the right direction.

You know you're a member of Club Grandma when . . .

—you carry a larger purse just to fit all the photos.
—you start exercising again—so you can lift the baby.
—you buy Christmas and Hanukkah presents all year round.
—your daughter answers the phone, "Hi Mom."

7.
Club Etiquette

Children divine those who love them;
it is a gift of nature which we lose as we grow up.
—Paul de Kock,
L'Hommes aux trois Culottes

The Queen Mother

When your first child is expecting, you are the Queen. It's a delightful time for flitting about, rejoicing, bragging and planning for the generation to come. Like all royalty, you bequeath your highest hopes on your future progeny.

The instant that baby is born, step aside. Smile while you do it, before someone gives you a shove whether you like it or not. Pass the baton graciously to the new Queen. You are now the Queen Mum!

Even though I've taught Child Development for most of my life, I truly believe that my daughter and son-in-law know the answers about their children's needs. Maybe that's because I was a Benjamin Spock mother. I met him once, in the British Virgin Islands. We were both sailing. We talked about children. Dr. Spock agreed that parents know their babies better than anyone else. Read the literature, consult the experts, but remember that your children know their children best.

Wait! Please don't disappear out the back door in all the fuss. Your role is far from over. You are the sage, wise in the ways of parenting that remain mysterious for those newly installed on the throne.

Let's try another example. . . . Let's say we're making a movie of your life. In Hollywood terms, you are now the producer, working behind the scenes to make this show happen. The new mother is the director, who bosses everyone around to accommodate her spin on the story. The new dad is the production designer, who sets the scene. The baby is the star. God writes the script. People in the know understand that there wouldn't be a movie without you.

Think Positive

Projection

How do you feel when someone refers to you as a wonderful grandmother? Anxious to hug and kiss your grandchildren, of course. What people project on to you, whether good or bad, often influences how you behave.

Two types of *negative projection* affect children strongly: the first is called "limiting." When Anne is referred to as the family athlete while Beth is described as the family artist, what are the odds that Anne will develop her drawing skills or that Beth will try out for swim team? Probably not so good. These kind of comments and comparisons are difficult to avoid, but they can severely limit your grandchildren's growth. Ultimately, it will hinder their success, which is based on both a child's self image and other people's expectations. Part of your role as a grandmother is to encourage your grandchildren to define themselves. Encourage them to explore all kinds of activities. Have them tell you their feelings about who they are and what they like by asking them questions and listening to their answers.

When I asked Juliette if she'd like to be a doctor, like her mother's friend, she said no. I asked her why not and she explained that she didn't want to give shots. So, I asked her what she did want to be. She said she wanted to be a teacher. Of course, that was last week.

The other kind of negative projection is "defining." The verse "sticks and stones may break my bones, but words can never hurt me" is entirely untrue. In fact, negative words *can* define a child, especially when it comes from an authority like Grandma. When Joey is accused of being a bad boy for hitting his friend, will he realize that it was only the act of hitting that was bad? Probably not. The real danger is that Joey may believe he is bad and live up to the title. This becomes a self-fulfilling prophesy. Always respond to a child's unwanted behavior by addressing the action, not the child. Words like stupid and idiot—even in jest—will stick, especially from you. The child may wrap his whole identity around that word. Say something nice, even when you're angry. "That was a bad thing to do, kiddo," or honey, cutie, jellybean—something. Anything!

Dr. Haim Ginott, the late child development expert, constantly reminded adults to let the child know "I love you, but I don't like your behavior." Here you are validating a child's self worth. Instead of insulting him, you are telling him that he is more valuable than the behavior itself, and you want to help him modify his behavior so he'll have a happier relationship with others.

68

The real issue at stake is self esteem—always build it up. Don't let your grandson see you wince at his new haircut. Remark on the fact that he got a haircut and ask if it was fun. Sidestep your negative opinion. If he corners you by asking how you like the haircut, tell him you think he's beautiful, inside and out.

Positive projection has a tremendous influence on children. Good, girl, smart girl, pretty girl, responsible girl—these kind of compliments will enhance your granddaughter's self image and help her to grow up good, smart, confident and responsible. It's equally important for children of both sexes.

A recent survey of women who are successful politicians revealed one very significant conclusion. These women grew up hearing how special they were. They were told, almost to the one, that they could accomplish anything they put their minds to. With few female role models on the political landscape, this is another illustration of how positive projection works.

Psychotherapy examines one's background by exploring the individual's experiences within the family system. My private practice draws individuals of all types involved in many different situations. When I ask my clients, men and women, "Who believed in you?" the answer is usually, "My grandmother."

Reflexive Listening

Forget the mumbo-jumbo; this is easier than it sounds. When your three-year-old mermaid proudly exclaims, "I swimmed across the pool the whole way!" repeat her sentence back with enthusiasm. Say, "You swam across the pool the whole way! That's wonderful!" The technique works with nearly any comment in any conversation. The child will be sure that you understand and really did hear her. This type of response validates both of you. As an extra bonus, she'll hear the corrected version of her sentence without being chided. After all, if she thinks she'll get an English lesson whenever she talks to you, most likely she'll stop talking.

This practice starts in infancy when a child points to a door, says door, and you repeat the word back to her. You may be surprised at the number of situations in which reflexive listening comes in handy—and not just with your grandchildren!

Miss Manners

Beware! Common sense can counteract the intentions of good manners. Children will be the first to notice. Every day we ask people how they are without really caring. Many times we don't even wait for an answer. So, if you tell your grandchildren that you've missed them, then ignore them, they'll naturally assume that you didn't miss them at all. But they won't chalk it up to good manners—they'll think you are a liar. And, the truth is, they'll be right. If you didn't miss them (maybe you just saw them yesterday), don't tell them you did. It's best to let your behavior be consistent with your words.

Becky, a friend of mine, is wistful about her grandmother, Sara. Sara refers to the grandchildren as jewels in her crown. Becky feels honored by this and she knows that Grandma Sara loves her. Whenever friends are around, Grandma Sara treats the children like diamonds. Becky used to love to dress up in the pretty clothes her Grandma brought and be paraded around the country club. However, that was pretty much the only time her Grandma paid any attention to her. You might say Becky got a mixed message . . . maybe Grandma Sara didn't really love her after all. Perhaps she just didn't know how to relate to a child; perhaps she was using them to enhance her own self worth. Whatever Sara's reason, take notice. Treat your grandchildren the same whether you are alone with them or in public. Be aware of their feelings. They are more than mere jewels in your crown.

If you brag about your grandchildren to others, yet fear complimenting them directly, it may be because you've heard that praise brings bad luck. Don't worry, that's an old wives tale. The reverse is true: praise is invaluable.

Grandchildren are the dividends of motherhood. You invested a lot of love and perspiration in raising your children, and your little heirs are a fair reward. Love can't spoil them. So, reinvest your love with theirs to help you both reap even greater dividends down the road.

Every Child Is Special

Each child deserves individual attention. Let her know that she is special all by herself. Emphasize what in particular makes her so special—from the color of her eyes, to her double-jointed thumb, to the way she loves to watch birds. When you must ask a child to wait until her brother is finished speaking or playing with you, remind her that she is just as special as he is and you want to give her every bit of your attention when it's her turn.

Feeling special builds security. Every child needs to feel safe within herself so that she can move on to trust the world around her. Only by truly understanding how special she is

71

can she learn as an independent self. Do you remember the joy on your child's face when she took her first steps? That is the joy of competency—the feeling of satisfaction from a job well done. Once a child feels emotionally secure, she can begin her journey towards autonomy. You can share the joy of your grandchild's first steps in the real world. Not only are you proud of her accomplishments; you are also partly responsible for her success. By making her feel special, you enable her to conquer the world.

Sibling Rivalry

New Baby

Do not—I repeat, do not—rush to the new baby! Restrain yourself. The baby will not remember this, but big brother will. He might even punish you for behaving so badly. He may withdraw every ounce of the cooperation that is essential to your relationship. You'll have to be patient to win him back and it won't be easy. Instead, emphasize what a wonderful big brother your grandson is, and how lucky his baby sister is to have him. Hug him, kiss him, give him a special "I'm a big brother" T-shirt. Then, go ahead and coo over the baby all you want!

Competition

Don't let siblings vie for your attention. Let them know that you have unlimited interest in each one of them, and taking turns lets you concentrate especially on them. When it comes to older children, it's best when gifts complement their individual interests. That way each child knows that you are paying attention and that you care specifically about him or her. With young children, similar or matching gifts are best to prevent any comparisons to discover who you like best. Competition can be healthy—but not when it comes to love.

Playing Favorites

Four generations were represented at Cody's birthday party. The birthday boy was the second of three great grandchildren. I was due to have my second child in another two weeks.

Cody's mother had her hands full with the party. I was in no condition to help, so I had the opportunity to sit and chat with the grandmother and great grandmother. Like many second-time Moms, I was nervous that I wouldn't have the same incredible amount of love for the new baby as I had for the first. The women assured me I would.

"What happens when it comes to grandchildren?" I asked.

"You automatically favor the first grandchild," replied Grandma.

Hmmm, I thought. We all watched the children for a moment. Then, Great Grandma spoke up. She didn't even look at her daughter; she just smiled at me.

"That's not true. You love them all equally." She turned to her daughter-in-law. "You're just a beginner. You'll see."

Nana holds the first one dear, but relates to my second baby because she, too, is a second child. Evidently, there will always be a reason for each child to be special.

Although being a favorite can make a child feel special, it creates too much pressure by keeping the child under a magnifying glass. It

73

can ultimately be too much to live up to. Each child is special in his or her own way.

Connect Creatively.

There are many ways to have an imaginative relationship with your grandchild. One way is to allow them the freedom to make choices about things when there is no one correct answer. For instance, you can let them choose what to have for lunch. With younger children, it's easiest for them if you limit their options. Feel free to suggest funny food combinations, like a peanut butter-spaghetti sauce sandwich. With older children, let them make the most out of this freedom by helping you make that peanut butter-spaghetti sauce sandwich. If it's truly ghastly, they won't eat it. If it's actually edible, they can catch up on their nutrition plan later. Either way, they'll love you for indulging their imaginations.

In our house, Nana asks Juliette to make choices for her baby sister. It's a powerful thing. This week, she decided that Catherine's favorite color is yellow, so that's what color balloon she gets. Until Catherine can let us know her true feelings, I think she enjoys having her sister standing up for her. Goodness knows, her big sister sure likes it!

Another way to use creativity in your relationship is to play make-believe games. Salvage those old clothes you can't part with, and maybe some of those you want to part with. Keep them in a trunk for the children's visits or send them off to their house. Not only will dress-up be fun, but it will remind them of you every time they play. Now, you might be thinking, "I'm not so self-centered that the children have to always be thinking of me." The truth is, it's healthy for them to think about you. As their grandma you represent security, roots and a positive connection to something larger than themselves. Maybe they'll make believe that they are you!

Go With the Flow

This is a tough one for me, even though I know it's important for everyone who deals with young children. I get so caught up trying to get everything on my list done, that when we plan a walk to the park, I make sure we get that accomplished, too. Fortunately, Nana is a pro. . . .

If you've planned something for the children's fun, yet they're enjoying something else on the way, why make them stop? If they are having a wonderful time picking up every twig and leaf on their slow motion walk, why make them hurry up to have fun someplace else? If lunch at Red Robin turns out to be a hit, does it matter if you miss the Children's Museum? If the only one who cares is you, let it go.

This also applies when it comes to toys. Just because the manufacturer had something specific in mind, that doesn't mean your grandchild should. As long as the toy has some sort of play value and the child is enjoying it, applaud the creative approach. Who says the colored rings must fit over the post? For now, maybe it's more fun teething on them, lining them up in a row or throwing them like Frisbees. Feel free to demonstrate how nicely they do stack on the post, in case it's not apparent, but let the child take over from there. Go with the flow.

You know you're a member of Club Grandma when . . .

— your sun visor doubles as a magic hat.
— the owner of the educational toy store sets things aside for you.
— you look forward to waking up early with your grandchildren.
— you buy Cheerios in bulk.
— your children count on you to help clean up before you leave.

8.

⬧ ⬧ ⬧ ⬧ ⬧ ⬧ ⬧

Club Privileges

*No cowboy was ever faster on the draw than a
grandparent pulling a baby picture out of a wallet.*
—Anonymous

*Privilege, noun: a special right, favor, etc.
granted to some person or group.*
Webster's New World Dictionary

I t is a privilege to be a grandmother, because nothing is
legally required of you. Different from automatic benefits, these are opportunities that are yours alone to take
advantage of. Remember, the more you give of yourself,
the more you'll be invited to share in the joys that children
offer.

Official Biographer

"Tell me a story!" cry the children, and what comes to mind?
Jack and Jill, The Three Pigs, Cinderella? How about real
stories that will make their eyes grow wide and your heart
beat pitter-pat? Tell them about your children. It will entertain
them more than make-believe, and it will help them see their
folks in a gentler light.

Tell them about your daughter's first visit from the Tooth
Fairy, when she cried because she wanted her tooth back. Tell
them about your son's third birthday party, when he smeared
cake all over his face. Stories like these will trigger warm
memories for you—things you may have forgotten. You'll

enjoy your children all over again. You'll remember the pains you went through to cheer up your daughter and how much trouble it was to make your son's clown-shaped cake. You'll feel pride at the considerate things you did. It will occur to you that, despite your natural misgivings, you really were a good parent.

You also have the opportunity to set the record straight. For years, I've pointed at our neighbor's Irish Setter and told my daughter that I had one when I was little. It was Nana who corrected my dwarfed view of history. The truth be told, Willie Wagtail was a Cocker Spaniel. I was so little, I assumed the dog was huge.

It's your privilege to fill in the parts of your children's lives that are exaggerated—or missing entirely. You can reinterpret events that will make a big impression on your grandchildren. When my mother saw Juliette abandon a game of musical chairs at a birthday party to look at the books in the birthday girl's room, she fueled our heredity versus environment discussion. I argued that Juliette sees us reading all the time; she pointed out that I did the same thing when I was young. Nana always wins . . . after all, she was there.

Wizard

I'll never forget the sparkling rubies hidden in the sand at my nursery school in Tucson. The director there was my surrogate grandma, and she told marvelous tales of how those rubies came to be. They were buried treasure, left by pirates. I can't remember the details, but I'll never forget the crystals, or that wonderful woman. Even though I know they might have just been some spilled beads, I wish I would have saved some, just in case. That sand was magical, and I think of it every time Juliette plays in the sand at her school.

Anything can be magical—you're the wizard, so you can decide. Can you make a perfect piece of cinnamon toast? Call it magic. Is there a silly dance step the women in your aerobics class perform? Call it a magic step and teach it to your grandchild. Is there an old scarf you don't wear, but can't bear to part with? Call it your magic scarf and let your grandchild wear it. It will help dry up tears from scraped knees and make any day special.

Nana always finds things in Juliette's ears. Big Bird lives there sometimes, and other times it's Minnie Mouse. Poor Juliette can never see for herself, but she trusts in Nana's words. Maybe you can do real tricks, like picking coins or candy out of your grandchildren's ears. Or, you can make things up. After all, there is no relationship more magical than yours.

What, You Again?

One of the privileges of being a grandma is that you can call your children as often as you like . . . as long as you ask for your grandchildren. In fact, if two days pass without a call from my mother, I start to worry. And it's great, because I never have to talk, unless I want to. I admit, sometimes I get jealous and demand my turn. Doesn't she want to know how *my* day went? This will work for you, too. Meanwhile, when your daughter sees Mommy stop everything to answer the phone—yet the call is for her, she will be thrilled.

There are always days when children don't want to talk; just send a message that you love them, hang up and call back another time. One day, when Juliette had already spoken with

Nana and the telephone rang once again, I handed the phone to Juliette and told her it was Nana. She shook her head and asked, "What, you again?" We're still laughing. Now it's one of Nana's favorite stories. And, believe me, she has a few.

Spitting Image

You call the shots in the looks department. Who does your grandchild really look like? Those aren't Daddy's ears, are they? No, they really came from your brother, the fireman. The brains, of course, came from you. Kids love to hear this stuff. It makes them proud. It gives them a sense of being part of a bigger picture. The mere shape of their chin connects them to other important people. Where did that dimple come from, anyway? I'll bet you know!

Sex Appeal

There are two popular caricatures of grandmothers: one shows a dumpy grandma with her hair in a silver bun, surrounded by screaming children; another shows a sexy thing holding a tennis racquet, with no time for kids. Most grandmas are somewhere in between. One privilege of being a grandma is that you can be as sexy as you want and still enjoy your grandchildren. Maybe you get lots of compliments when you go out—no need to pretend you are so young that it comes naturally. Now you earn added respect, because you're a grandma and you still look great.

You don't have to dress conservatively to be a "proper" mother anymore. Social taboos are behind you, whether you paid attention or not. There is something inherently sexy about motherhood. It's proof of sexuality, after all. Think how sexy this makes you . . . even your children have procreated. Sex is not a dirty word. It's the word that got us all here. Enjoy.

Shop 'Till You Drop

Finally an excuse to shop anywhere, any time, for anything! It makes no difference whether you're at Saks Fifth Avenue, K Mart, or the corner grocery store. There's always a sale on something. Your grandchildren are always going to need bigger clothes, party shoes, a funny T-shirt, a new kite, a pop-up book, a cute greeting card, a fresh pack of gum . . . the list is endless.

Are you the kind of mother who, when your daughter admired your earrings, you gave them to her? If so, this generous trait will manifest itself into more trouble with your grandchildren. A word of warning here . . .

> *Beware the slip of the tongue. Last week, my granddaughter admired my yellow shoes. Automatically, I told her I'd buy her some to match. Now, I'll have to follow through. Spending the extra money is one thing. Finding canary yellow shoes in toddler size 10½ is another. Next time, I'll just give her a kiss and say thank-you.*

Now is not the time to break the bank—next week the folks might hit you up for a new bicycle. Nevertheless, if you've got a dime, there's a stick of licorice with your grandchild's name on it just waiting for you!

You know you're a member of Club Grandma when . . .

— you decide you can do without the new handbag—your granddaughter absolutely must have that darling pinafore.

— your arms feel empty and you know it's time for a visit.

— you feel beautiful, crows feet and all.

— you know the names of the Teenage Mutant Ninja Turtles.

9.
⊛ ⊛ ⊛ ⊛ ⊛ ⊛ ⊛
I.D. Cards

A grandma is old on the outside and young on the inside.
—John Wright, age 7½

Who Are You?

Name, Rank and Serial Number

I t's Friday afternoon and you're at the bank. You left your automatic teller card in your other purse so you have to withdraw cash the old fashioned way. You pass the time reading New Accounts literature. The line shifts. You look up and catch the eye of the young teller at window #4. He smiles. You smile back and try to concentrate on that scintillating brochure. Meanwhile, you wonder if your hair is brushed. When is the last time you freshened your lipstick? What are you wearing? What exactly did he see when he looked at you? Do you look like a Grandma?

You get your cash from a different teller then go home and realize you forgot to check if that last deposit cleared. You look at the clock—the bank is just closing. Frantically, you look up the bank's phone number and dial it. The man who answers was the teller at window #4. You identify yourself with your name, rank and serial number: Judith Littleton, checking customer, account #777777. Does he know it's you? He sounds tired, and you're feeling friendly, but who are you to him, really? More importantly, who are you to you?

When you look in the mirror, who do you see? Forget the

physical factors, they're transient. Who is behind those intelligent eyes?

Make a list of words that describe you. It might look like this:

corporate CEO
wife
feminist
friend
lover
intellectual
athlete
movie buff
bowling pro
shower opera singer
seamstress
championship shopper
gourmet chef
sister
mother
grandmother

Now, put those words in order of importance. The order may change from day to day. The significant ones won't. Examine your list.

These days, when many people start their own families in their thirties, motherhood lasts a pretty long time. So, it's likely that you see yourself as a mother, first and foremost. Your business role is important and has ego prominence, yet motherhood comes from the heart. But, like Hollywood says about classic films, you have transcended the genre. You've done motherhood one better. You are a grandma. Put it at the top of your list!

"Grandma" Means Power

Vanity Fair magazine introduced a former mayor in President Clinton's administration as a "grandmother of three." The game show "Wheel of Fortune" described a business owner as a "grandmother" before listing her professional credentials. This is not meant to demean these accomplished women by bringing them down to a stereotypical female role; on the contrary, this identity gives you status in society. As a grandparent, you have roots in the past and influence on the future. You have power!

If you are on the telephone with that anonymous bank teller and you mention that you are a brain surgeon, the young man might be impressed. He might be envious of your bank balance. He might wonder how you deal with all that blood. On the other hand, if you introduce yourself as a grandmother, he will hold you in esteem and think of his own grandmother. He will assume you are wise, capable of great love, and that you care about the world. If he knows you are a grandmother, you will get better service!

Mirror, Mirror

Relax, the pressure's off. It doesn't really matter what you look like anymore. In fact, a friend of mine's kids were embarrassed to bring their grandma to Grandparents Day at school, because she didn't look like a "real" grandma—she was too young and pretty! At any rate, please yourself. You no longer have to compete with women whom gravity has never touched. Everyone's underarms will sag at some point. After all, you are a grandma now—it's not your toned thighs that attract adoration. It's you.

If you are young and beautiful, don't fret over the title—especially with the children. If they hear you say you are too young to be a grandmother, they will figure you don't like them. After all, they know you are a grandma. If you love them, how could you be too young? Besides, it's fun to be a young grandma. You have the energy to keep up! Our Nana didn't truly start an exercise regime until after Juliette was born.

My arms used to hurt from carrying the baby, so I started a weight training regime—and met other grandmas doing the same thing. Now I want to stay in shape to make my girls proud. Mostly, I want to stay healthy so I can enjoy a long, happy life with my grandchildren.

Just between you and me, I suspect she also wants to fit into matching grandma/granddaughter outfits!

The New You

How many times have you heard the word eccentric paired with grandmother? It's a natural outgrowth of living long enough and gaining the self-confidence to do whatever you damn please. (Excuse the language, "darn" just isn't strong enough to describe being free at last.) With this identity comes liberation. No longer must you endure your children's harsh scrutiny. No longer do you have to dress respectably for the P.T.A. As a grandma, it's your job to be fun and to have fun! Grandchildren don't embarrass easily. Now is your chance to greet the mailman in your bathrobe. Now is your chance to wear that silver studded purple denim skirt, if that's your taste. Heck, Elizabeth Taylor does it! Now is your chance to try skydiving. Didn't Clare Booth Luce scuba dive during her eighties? It's time to please yourself. Let your children shake their heads and sigh, if they must. They are past being disgraced by you—now they can be amused. Like the song says—don't worry, be happy!

Qualifications

Your Club Grandma Identification Card is proof that you've made it through the rough parts of life. You've raised your family and worked hard for many years. You may or may not be working still. You have vast experience and a genuine stake in the world. You have fulfilled your genetic imperative by producing future generations. Hold your head high. Flash that membership card. You're a grandma!

You know you're a member of Club Grandma when . . .

—your daughter-in-law is still not good enough, but she looks better all the time.
—you stop worrying about grey hair.
—your grandson has a tantrum and you insist that it simply shows his independent spirit.
—you go on vacation with the grandchildren even if it means putting up with their parents all week.
—you trade your floral stationery for postcards with animals.

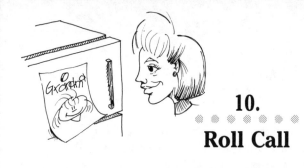

10.
Roll Call

Grandparents don't have to be smart—only answer questions like why dogs hate cats and how come God isn't married.
—Patsy Gray, age 9

What's Your Style?

Around the country, women are lining up to be grandmas. It's the latest craze! Indeed, there are almost as many kinds of grandmas as there are women. Let's see if you can find your type . . .

East Coast Grandma

Dress: Always in stockings or grey flannel trousers, the ultimate in sophistication, she has a standing appointment at the hairdresser.

Gifts: Mock Chanel suits and manicure kits to the girls; suspenders and hockey sticks to the boys.

Playtime: Natural history museum for the dinosaur exhibit; Carnegie Hall for the children's matinee.

Upon Hearing the News: Gets a certified illustration of the family tree matted, framed and hung in the foyer.

Baby Blanket: Handmade in Europe or Hackensack.

Breakfast: Croissants or bagels with fresh squeezed orange juice.

Favorites: Loves to be compared to a mother duck with her adorable ducklings following her all in a line.

88

West Coast Grandma

Dress: Usually blonde, she wears dangling earrings that the baby loves to play with and revels in leggings and oversized T-shirts.

Upon Hearing the News: Installs a child's seat on her bicycle.

Gifts: Mickey Mouse T-shirts, brightly colored sunblock, Boogie boards and Frisbees.

Playtime: Finger painting and collecting seashells.

Baby Blanket: Only the best for baby—Baby Dior from the local department store.

Homemade Breakfast: Fruit salad and seven grain toast.

Favorites: Loves to be mistaken for the children's mother.

Southern Grandma

Dress: Has five pairs of white pants, keeps hair short or pulled back with a ribbon and wears novelty earrings in the shape of alligators and cows.

Gifts: Sundresses with matching hats and jump ropes for girls, sneakers and fishing rods for boys.

Playtime: Gardening and card games.

Upon Hearing the News: Calls on all the neighbors with homemade jam.

Breakfast: Sunny-side-up eggs and hominy grits.

Baby Blanket: Baby sized quilt, made with friends.

Favorites: Loves to take them to town and introduce them everywhere.

Northern Grandma

Dress: Monogrammed sweater and penny loafers with nickels in them, same hairdo since college (usually pageboy).

Gifts: Orders monogrammed jumpers from catalogs, matching mitten and hat sets for everyone, plus box kites like when she was a girl.

Playtime: Hide & seek and watching "The Wizard of Oz."

Upon Hearing the News: Starts putting together a care package of baby toiletries, digs out the family Christening gown.

Breakfast: Oatmeal, fresh blueberry muffins and frozen juice.

Blanket: Hand knit by the fire.

Favorites: Loves family gatherings: plans for Thanksgiving all year round.

Midwest Grandma

Dress: Gray hair and designer warm-up suit.

Gifts: Big Ten sweatshirts, red wagons and sleds.

Playtime: Feeding the animals, reading books at bedtime.

Upon Hearing the News: Holds neighborhood brunch to announce news publicly.

Breakfast: Fresh pancakes with lots of sausage.

Blanket: Hand-crocheted during "All My Children."

Favorites: Loves to have everybody in matching red, white, and blue outfits on the Fourth of July.

Southwest Grandma

Dress: Silver and turquoise jewelry, espadrilles and jeans.

Gifts: Moccasins, cowboy hats and board games.

Playtime: "I Spy" during sunrise walks.
Upon Hearing the News: Fixes air conditioning, finally, for the
   baby's visit.
Breakfast: Pasoles and scrambled eggs.
Blanket: Woven Indian papoose blanket from the nearby reser-
   vation.
Favorites: Loves to sketch her grandchildren in oil pastels.

How Do Your Grandchildren See You?

To see what you really look like, ask your grandchildren to
draw you a picture. The proverb is true: a picture really is
worth a thousand words.

   Children are first capable of drawing faces between the
ages of three and four. Once the young artists mature and their
hand-eye coordination is honed they learn to add more details.
Nevertheless, arms, legs, eyelashes and clothing will not
change the essence of your portrait. The differences between
children's artwork depends less on each child's specific talents, and more on the how each child understands the
subject . . . how they see you in their mind's eye. The real
contrast between two children's portraits will be determined
by your relationship.

   Ideally, your face will be full and round. Your eyes will be
open and your mouth will be smiling. It doesn't matter if you
have a body or not, as long as you fill most of the page. When
this child thinks of you, you are the center of the universe. If
you are on the left side of the page, there is a strong
attachment, but your likeness is drawn from a hazy memory.
Your image is likely borrowed from grandmothers in books or
on television. If your picture is very small or your face is in
profile, the relationship has little to draw on . . . literally.

Sometimes a child will draw a doll or puppet figure with old fashioned clothes and no expression. This means he can only imagine Grandma. It's time to pick up the phone.

As an experiment, I asked Juliette to draw a picture of Nana. Her hair was yellow, her face was a huge circle with round eyes and a U-shaped smile. Next, I asked her to draw a picture of Grandma Jean. Juliette only met Grandma Jean once, when she was a tiny infant. She sees the family photograph of her grandma holding her when we lift her up in the hallway to look. She has also seen pictures in our scrapbook. She knows Grandma Jean has been in Heaven for a long time now. Since this relationship was so brief, I expected a pretend grandma in the picture. She asked me what Grandma Jean's hair looked like, then proceeded to draw another big happy face. Scrambling, I called my mother. . . .

> *"Mom, Juliette just disproved all my research! Maybe I should scrap this chapter. She drew Grandma Jean almost the same as you."*
>
> *"Those studies are still accurate, Leslie," my mother explained, "Juliette has a good relationship with me. All the data she has received about Grandma Jean has been positive as well. You've validated that relationship in her mind through memories and photographs. She has no reason to have any empty or negative feelings about her late grandmother."*

So, according to my resident expert, Juliette reinforced these conclusions by illustrating that a positive relationship with one grandmother can influence her feelings about grandmothers in general.

Psychologists use pictures a great deal when working with young children. They concentrate on their developing small motor ability to draw recognizable forms, rather than the picture's style or content. In other words, children are not sophisticated enough to fabricate an image. Their pictures don't lie. So, don't ask for a portrait unless you truly want one. If you get a big happy face . . . frame it!

Just Nana

Come see the amazing, stupendous and fantastic, truly incredible Super Grandma! Don't turn the page—I was just kidding. What's wrong, are you feeling a little guilty? Nervous, maybe? Worried that your true talents might not fit the bill? Or exhausted already from trying to be this woman? Don't worry, Super Grandma is a hard image to live up to. In fact it's impossible . . . and unnecessary.

Face it, you are incredibly talented at a number things. But not everything. Fortunately, you don't have to be the best at everything. You don't even have to try everything. Remember that old adage, "jack of all trades, master of none"? You undoubtedly have your share of talents. After all, there are other things in your life besides being a grandmother. Many of these things will add zest to the love you have to offer your grandchildren.

Perfection is not the goal. Not for you, and not for your grandchild. You don't have to teach him his manners, ballroom dancing and the French language. There is no need to try so hard, to know all things, teach all things and be all things. Simply offer what you know. The goal is to have a good relationship. Relax and enjoy each other.

Most people have a treasured memory of one special time spent with grandma. My mother's friend, Suzanne, yearns to return to that summer afternoon singing songs while her grandma brushed her hair. She remembers being told how her hair shone and how beautifully she sang. She remembers feeling that her grandmother would have loved her hair and her singing no matter what—because her grandma loved *her* no matter what. She felt especially close to her Grandma that day, and realized that she loved her grandma no matter what, as well.

When asked about their favorite memories of grandparents, adult grandchildren have similar answers in almost every case. They relive time spent just relaxing and talking with their grandparents, getting to know them . . . and getting to love them. (This may explain why fishing is so popular.) What is your favorite memory of your Grandma? What do you want your grandchildren to remember . . . you? Share yourself.

Nature Versus Nurture

Nature's role is predetermined. Those chromosomes are pretty darn influential. In fact, if you have a daughter, your genetic power is even clearer: her baby's genes were partially formed while she was inside you. So, you've already done that part. Now it's time for your true role: nurturer.

What do you think of when "grandma" comes to mind? The old-fashioned vision of a soft, aproned woman with long grey hair wound into a bun, stirring a steaming pot and removing a sheet of sticky buns from the oven? Maybe that doesn't describe you—but it is, believe it or not, what you're all about.

The greatest human needs are food, clothing and shelter. Notice the order these fall in: food is number one. Food equals love . . . especially to children. Food shouldn't replace love or it could lead to eating disorders. So, perhaps we should consider food as an accessory to love. After all, romance is usually sparked by a candlelight dinner, n'est ce pas? Food is the easiest and most obvious way to express your love. It provides sustenance of the most basic sort. Therefore, this traditional stereotype of grandmother in the kitchen is not a threat to you. On the contrary, it reinforces your very essence. It follows that the kitchen is an honorable place.

Those legendary family dinners may be a relic of our collective past, but you can still feed your grandchildren. If you don't like to cook, so what? A child won't care that the reason your cupboard is bare is because you don't have the time to cook. He'll only see that his friends' grandmas feed them and you don't. So, in his mind, you must not love him.

It's easy to fulfill this bare minimum requirement for grandmothers: keep your cupboards stocked. As long as you have some version of Cheerios, apple juice, chocolate pudding and hugs, your grandchildren will know you to be "The Great Nurturer." You can be a legend in your own time.

You know you're a member of Club Grandma when . . .

—you dress in green because it's your grandchild's favorite color.
—you are paying for ballet lessons—again.
—your daughter wants to visit (with the kids).
—you'd rather dine with a three-year-old than with an eligible bachelor.
—you know why little girls are named Ariel, Belle, and Jasmine.

11.

⊛ ⊛ ⊛ ⊛ ⊛ ⊛ ⊛ ⊛

Clubhouse

A grandmother is a babysitter
who watches the kids instead of television.
—Anonymous child, age 6

Your Home

I your first reaction to becoming a grandparent was fear for the sanctity of your home, don't despair. Go ahead, pack up all your crystal and everything else that's breakable, valuable, sentimental, small, sharp or poisonous. Cover your couches with blanket throws, indefinitely postpone the white Berber carpet and put that *Architectural Digest* back on the book shelf. In fact, maybe you *should* fear for the sanctity of your home!

It wasn't until I had my first baby that I understood why my paternal grandmother's furniture was always covered in plastic. Plastic was "hip" in the sixties, so I had assumed it was some kind of a fashion statement. Other grandmothers were famous for their creative use of cloth doilies. If these ideas sound like a good way to save your furniture, be sure you know what it is you are saving the furniture for. In any case, if you plan on having your grandchildren around, either the place will have to change or your designer dreams will.

There is a happy medium. Do baby-proof for the baby's safety and kid-proof for your own peace of mind. Then take a deep breath and expect the worst. Reality may be terrifyingly close, but at least you'll be relaxed about it. If you're too nervous to enjoy the children, then the children will be nervous, too. After all, nobody likes to hang out at the Frick Museum. It's great for short, formal visits, but there's no place comfortable to sit, you can't touch anything past your nose (which is frowned upon) and you certainly can't bring your lunch. You want your grandchildren to visit . . . so, you'll adapt. It'll only be another fifteen years until you can unpack that Ming vase. Think how much more it will be worth then. Of course, by then, you might not care.

Here are some specific tips to help both you and the kids feel at home:

1. *Keep some toys on hand.* Nothing big, nothing expensive, just some generic stuff to keep the children busy when there's still ten minutes before dinner and they're bored of the twenty-eight toys they brought with them. Animal puppets are great because you can get involved—this little bit of effort goes a long way in the children's estimation of grandma. No need to try to be a ventriloquist for children under ten—they are more interested in your imagination than your method. Crayons and paper are a perennial favorite because children can play by themselves, plus you can always assign them a particular picture to extend the activity. Puzzles and colorful building blocks are also a safe bet. (Be sure to avoid small pieces less than 1 1/2 inches long with children under 3.) Best of all, a six- to eight-inch ball will be popular with every age group and will also help get the whole brood out of the house for a little while.

2. *Stop at the video store before your grandchildren's arrival.* Get some wholesome cartoons or a family movie that you're familiar with to help fill those restless hours before bedtime. Never trust the ratings labels on movies! Many popular movies that are marketed for children have strong language and violence in them. Even though they may watch it at their house, parents aren't always completely aware of the contents.

More importantly, it doesn't mean you have to condone it. There are plenty of other options. Ask the clerk in the store. Better yet, now might be the perfect time to meet the young parents down the block.

3. *Don't spend too much time cleaning up before the big visit.* This sparkling visage won't last long and you'll just have to do it again when they leave. If the visit is short and you have gifts for the children that don't fall into the clothing category, save one as a reward for helping you clean up. That way, they'll spend those precious hours focusing on you, not just the new toys—plus they'll have something fresh and exciting to remember you by.

4. *If you have time to grocery shop, find out what they like to eat.* Now is not the time to train them to eat properly. Sure, have some vegetables and dip as a fun, healthy alternative. But if they really love macaroni and cheese for dinner, don't bother with liver and onions. It's not worth the effort or the smell. Remind the parents to bring the multi-vitamins or keep some handy. Keep spaghetti and other easy meals on hand. Taking the crowd out to eat takes twice as much time, money, discipline, discomfort and laundry.

5. *You do not have to clear your schedule completely.* If the visit is for several days, invite the kids along to your tennis game. Suggest alternative activities while you use those theater tickets you ordered months ago. Take turns: bring your grandson and his new book with you to the hairdresser and then take him to the train exhibit. Let your granddaughter have a manicure. Visit that sick friend during nap time (if their parents are there to watch them). Have that out-of town friend visit *you* for a half hour. Children need to respect that grandma has a life too. They need to know that even with all your activities, your favorite time is with them.

6. *If possible, keep a high chair and crib at your place for overnight visitors.* It's a heck of a lot easier than bringing them,

renting them or not having them—and it might lead to more frequent visits. Discount stores have lots of baby sales. The new high chairs are padded, easy to clean and fold up nicely to fit in the closet. You may find great deals at garage sales and consignment stores, but be wary. Always keep safety standards in mind when buying used baby equipment—even from friends. Don't get anything damaged or old. Safety standards are updated constantly as accidents are reported. Go to the library and read *Consumer Reports* or call the manufacturer's Customer Service department.

7. *Always use car seats!* Not only are they required by law, but in fatal traffic accidents, it's usually the infant in the car seat who survives. Like skiing, most accidents happen on the home stretch—when you're tired and your guard is down because home is just around the corner. This is the biggest challenge with my mother. When I was little, she'd deposit me in the car and away we'd go. What can I say, there was less traffic then maybe less accurate accident statistics. That argument doesn't justify the danger. Just make it a habit to use infant seats, booster seats and seat belts.

8. *Never leave children unattended.* Not when you run into the dry cleaners, not when the phone rings, never! Take the kids with you. Use safety straps. Count on the worst. Newborns can squirm and fall out of infant seats. Babies can choke just resting on your bed. Toddlers drown in bathtubs and toilets—it really happens. Ten-year-olds can find that loose nail—in their foot. Teenagers can slice their fingers instead of sandwiches. It pays to be paranoid!

Their Home

1. *Keep an open mind.* The experts say that if a toddler's house is immaculate, then something is terribly amiss. People are

more important than things. If you can't stand the mess—or it's more than simple clutter—ask before you roll up your sleeves and clean up. Uninvited cleaning may be taken as an insult. Be a blessing, not a burden. Smile and be glad it's not your place.

2. *Gifts are not required.* If you can't resist, here is a suggestion: avoid sweets. Parents have enough trouble controlling children's nutritional intake—don't add additional stress unless you make it clear this is a special treat for after dinner. If you can't think of anything spectacular, but don't want to show up empty-handed, bring fun and useful items like blowing bubbles, sidewalk chalk or character toothbrushes. Think educational with a fun twist, like musical or pop-up books.

If you can't resist that adorable pinafore or the athletic shoes with blinking lights, make sure the tags are on them. Offer the parents the receipts. It is true that a child can stay dormant for months then grow an inch in twenty-four hours! The children may not fit in the clothes, they may already have these items or they may be in dire need of something else. For teenagers, money is always appreciated. If it's five dollars, let them spend it on themselves and have fun. If it's twenty dollars, talk to them about saving up for that new bike. That way it's a lesson in disguise.

3. *Participate in activities with them.* Get down on the floor and roll the ball to the baby, make animals with clay alongside the toddler, play dolls or color with the school children, etc. Sneak in a little fresh air and exercise by asking the older children to take a walk with you and show you where their friends live . . . or take a "listening" walk where you describe the sounds you hear and what makes them. Influence good reading habits by reading stories to them, taking them to the library and buying them special interest magazines and,

yes, even comic books. Plan a big event for your visit that everyone can look forward to, then remember when you are gone. For the little ones, this may mean a simple park outing; the older ones may be anxious to see the new Disney movie or visit the Harvest Festival. You don't have to take them places by yourself—you just have to be there to share the experience.

4. Baby-sitting can be fun for the parents and the children—and yes, even for you. Be sure to get a list of do's and don'ts: remember the safety rules then ignore the rest! Knowing that you are breaking the rules is a lot more fun than winging it.

With older kids, lay down your own ground rules for peace of mind. Then offer freedom within that structure. Be an accomplice—let them stay up late—and order pizza! There will be no harm done and the parents will be so grateful for the free night and late-sleeping, happy kids, that they won't complain a bit. They probably expected it, anyway.

You know you're a member of Club Grandma when . . .

— you pull money out of your retirement savings to buy toys.
— you look forward to ballet recitals.
— you install a crib in your den.
— you understand why people use plastic slipcovers on couches.

12.

❊ ❊ ❊ ❊ ❊ ❊ ❊ ❊ ❊

Entertainment Committee

*Being grandparents sufficiently removes us
from the responsibilities so that we can be friends—
really good friends.*
—Dr. Allan Frome, pediatrician

Special Events

Every occasion with grandma is a special one. Yet, it doesn't hurt to make sure that everyone feels the same way. Odd as it may seem, the best way to make events particularly special is to make a tradition of doing them with you. When you have a regular activity that you do with your grandchildren, you are the one who makes it special.

If you live nearby, you can join a Mommy & Me class with the baby and make it your regular—special—outing. You can be the one who takes the kids to the new Disney film each time one opens. You can take them to dancing or to martial arts lessons.

If you live far away from your grandchildren, how about planning ahead for the ball game or the concert in the park or even the circus? At our house, Nana takes the girls to Mc-Donalds for breakfast. Julliette calls it "Ol' McDonalds" and Catherine calls it "Eeyieeyio" so they have a tradition of singing all the way there. Afterwards, they run wild in the restaurant playground.

When we're at Nana's, Juliette's special event is feeding the ducks at the nearby pond. Sometimes, the rest of the family joins them. When Nana is busy, I take Juliette. But I'm just a visitor—it's their thing. It's still the special event that Juliette relates to Nana. That's what always makes it so special.

Whether it's twice a year or twice a month, as long as you share the activity on a consistent basis, almost anything will fit the bill.

Family Dining

Do you love to eat out? If so, it's only natural that you'll want to go out with your growing clan. Here's a typical scenario: at first, you'll play Queen Mum and pay for everyone. This is a generous attitude and you'll all have a wonderful time. By the second time, the credit card bill for the first meal will have arrived, and you might be a tad less enthusiastic. Your son-in-law will probably be anxious to pay this time, but you'll overrule him and say it's your pleasure. By the third time, you will be reluctant to mention eating out and will be grateful when your daughters suggests you all go out "on them." Now whenever you go out, it is assumed the children will pay. But you are getting worried about their finances, and frankly, so are they.

The solution? Establish an understanding that everyone will pay their own way. Simply state that you (and your husband) will contribute your share. You can skirt the issue by asking if twenty dollars will cover you or, if they plan to use a credit card, can you write them a check? This way, it is obvious that you plan to pay and your only concern is not being caught short. If you simply ask how much money you'll need, they will probably be polite and say don't worry about it, they'll pay. Don't let them, or they may not want to go out next time.

If the restaurant is your choice, advise them about the

price of meals before getting your coat. Ask if your favorite Italian eatery will be all right. If they don't seem enthusiastic, either volunteer to pay more than your share or suggest the less expensive Mexican place around the corner. This way, you can go out whenever you want without any resentment or guilt. If one party is feeling flush they can play host by contributing as much extra as they want to the bill. The same goes for take-out meals. The most important thing to remember is to confirm the payment plan in the same breath as the restaurant suggestions.

Obviously, if one party lacks the means, the other should pick up the slack. Birthdays and other celebrations are a good excuse for somebody to pick up the whole tab—but it's not written in stone. Do whatever feels comfortable.

With young grandchildren, you will probably visit a lot more hamburger joints than anywhere else. That's okay. It is important to take the children out so they can learn restaurant etiquette early. Just don't expect them to behave like little adults—they are not. Bring toys and crayons and patience. Avoid going at naptime and bedtime. Plan a tour of the restaurant to stretch those little legs and burn off some of the energy that would drive everyone crazy if it stayed pent-up in the booth.

Family meals at home can be a struggle as well. If you can, offer to help with groceries at their house, but do take "no" for an answer. For a meal at your house, ask them to pick up something specific, like beverages and dessert or a fresh flower centerpiece. It's easier than dividing up the cost of a large family meal. Bartering for clean-up chores may be acceptable to everyone. Another alternative is to set out a bowl for contributions. It's as close as you'll get to anonymous donations, and the collective consciousness is sure to cover the tab.

Money is not a dirty word as long as you keep it out in the open. Once you can talk about it, you'll all have more fun.

Vacations

With the Family

A friend of mine, Kim, had the good fortune to go to Hawaii on vacation this year. Her family was sharing a condo with her brother's family. She took along her 13-year-old baby-sitter to help with the three children, all under the age of four. I was green with envy. She agreed that the situation was pretty good, but it could have been better. She told me about a family on the plane who vacationed in style. Their baby-sitter dealt with the kids in Coach while the parents enjoyed the luxury of First Class. To me this was beyond a good idea—it was fantasy land.

The possibilities simmered in my mind for several days. I planned how I would do it and what the perfect conditions would entail. I thought about what baby-sitter I would bring. Could she be trusted in a strange place? How much time off would she need? Wouldn't she just be another child to be responsible for? What if we brought our part-time house-keeper? Would we be comfortable living with her for a week? We'd have to pay for her trip and expenses—how much salary would we have to pay? I thought about it and thought about it.

When the children are older, we could solve the vacation riddle by going to a hotel with a children's activity schedule. But for now, the situation seemed desperate. Then it dawned on me. My mother fit all my requirements, met all my concerns—and would be more fun. Plus, she'd enjoy the vacation.

Hawaii was out of the question. Instead, we decided to

drive down to La Jolla, near San Diego, for a long weekend. Mom was raring to go. She offered to pay for her room and we quickly agreed to pay for everything else. We got adjoining rooms—guess who the kids wanted to sleep with? The first few days were blissful. We played on the beach together and took turns doing whatever we were in the mood for. There was always someone who wanted to go inside while the baby napped. My husband and I went out to dinner by ourselves and took romantic walks on the beach. The children were safe and happy. We could all be grouchy when we felt like it. We took advantage of Nana—without taking advantage of her. She gave us breathing room. When Nana got sick of us, she took a long walk and disappeared . . . for three hours. By the time she returned, she was refreshed and we were starting to miss her.

After a few days we were all ready to go off to our respective homes. When the car broke down on the freeway, we pretty much hit our vacation low. Mom directed questions at me that were actually intended for my husband. Then she got eerily quiet. I was sick of her. My husband was irritable. The baby was teething. Our three-year-old was hot and cranky. We'd all had enough of each other.

A few days later, I overheard my husband telling a friend about our vacation. Uh-oh, I thought, here it comes. "That's right, my mother-in-law," he said, "My motto is 'Nana: don't leave home without her!'"

The moral of the story is, no family vacation is ideal, but with grandma it's close. Volunteer to go on vacation with your grandchildren. If you are married or involved, you'll need to work out the logistics with your mate. Either way, keep these points in mind: you're better than a babysitter, you'll share a memorable experience with the children and you might get a free vacation out of it.

Without the Family

Nana dreams of taking the girls on world cruises with her. She wants to travel the Orient, visit the Louvre and relax in the Caribbean with her granddaughters. She wants to share the world with them. Maybe you <u>sent</u> your children to Europe or the Grand Canyon. Wouldn't you rather <u>take</u> your grandchildren?

Vacationing with your grandchildren can be a wonderful experience. They are away from parental pressures and so are you. You'll have a constant companion who looks up to you and follows your lead. You can revisit places with a fresh perspective. You can explore new places as you never imagined them. Or you can relax and enjoy your grandchild's company in a fun environment where bedtimes don't matter and you don't have to make the beds.

Most resort hotels now offer children's programs, so you don't have to be responsible for 24-hour entertainment. You can both have a good time and meet new friends. *The Los Angeles Times* recently devoted the entire travel section to family cruises, available from many of the cruise lines. The RFD Travel Corporation offers tour packages specifically for grandparents and grandchildren (ages eight to sixteen) to explore America together. Not only can you rediscover your heritage, but you can personally introduce your heirs to their ancestors. Visit your travel agent or call the Auto Club and map out your own road trip. Plan a vacation that you and your grandchild will never forget!

You know you're a member of Club Grandma when . . .

— strange children talk to you in public places.
— your son considers you an authority.
— your favorite jewelry is plastic.
— you love home movies.

13.

⊛ ⊛ ⊛ ⊛ ⊛ ⊛ ⊛

Family Politics

To reform a man, you must begin with his grandmother.
—Victor Hugo

Did you marry for love? If you are royalty, then probably not. In fact, most marriages before this century were planned by people who had ulterior motives for uniting couples. Lives were arranged to further business and political pursuits. The union of two people could ally opposing clans. The birth of a baby could prevent a war.

Even now, a new baby can bring a family together in peace. You can be the facilitator. There is no need to declare the winner of the historical disagreement between your Hatfields and McCoys. You don't even need to negotiate a truce. Simply ignore the strained communications and start a peaceful new era. A grandchild gives relatives something in common. After all, someone new has their blood. Let your enthusiasm for the new baby draw the family close.

Extended Family

Send birth announcements! If the proud parents are spreading the news, put your order in for a dozen additional cards. Lure them with the likelihood of more gifts by reminding them to get thank-you notes as well. Offer to do the family announcements, or to help with all the addresses. Some mothers like to do this alone as a rite of passage—it makes a personal situation real in terms of the outside world. Most parents will be so overwhelmed—especially with the first child—that they'll welcome your help.

Last week I received an announcement from an old friend whose baby was born ten days earlier. I was amazed how fast Lisa accomplished the social niceties. When I called, her mother-in-law answered the phone. I knew they had a respectfully distant relationship. Lisa picked up the phone and explained how her mother-in-law was so excited about the baby that she flew in without her husband, rolled up her sleeves and got to work. Lisa's mother-in-law had sent out the announcements! It was the start of a new relationship for all of them. It doesn't matter who pays for the postage or where the postmarks are stamped, this is a fun way to be helpful.

On a Sunday, soon after the announcements are mailed, get out your phone book. People will be relaxed at the end of a weekend, and the phone rates will be low. Feel free to call cousins you haven't heard from in years. No one can cast doubt on the excitement of a grandmother—no matter how many grandchildren you have. It is always special. Mention how the baby's chin reminds you of them. Offer to send a photograph. Ask for phone numbers and addresses of others—for more announcements or for your Christmas card list. Even remote relatives are bound to feel more connected. Once you are in touch, it's your decision whether or not to stay in touch. At least, make the first effort. Maybe one day soon, they'll call you.

In-Laws and Outlaws

Now is a good time to get to know your married children's in-laws. You are bound to be thrown together on family occasions from here on out—why not get to know each other first? Holidays are stressful times even when relationships are smooth; you can make them go that much smoother by eliminating the additional challenge of getting along with the in-laws. Relatives are given, not chosen, and in this case the only thing you may have in common is your children. Inviting them for coffee or a commemorative glass of champagne will initiate a new relationship that may offer you things you never would have imagined. At least make the effort. If it doesn't work out so well, maybe it's because they are shy or afraid. Maybe they just need more time. What do you have to lose? Nothing. On the contrary, you'll have gained the edge for those grandchildren's birthday parties. You'll be able to smile easily. After all, you tried.

Competition is healthy in many arenas . . . the family is not one of them. Avoid forcing your children to choose between your house and their house for Thanksgiving. Offer an alternative holiday, or ask if you can join them. When you have many family members to consider, it helps to plan ahead.

With the children, the competition can get nasty. The fact that your in-laws bought the playhouse doesn't mean you have to splurge for a swing set. This is not a contest for the affection of your grandchildren. Go along with the program. Buy a child-sized chair for the playhouse. How about a plastic phone or rake? Children don't keep score. Often, little ones enjoy playing with the boxes more than the gifts. You may find that a simple jump rope will turn out to be the favored toy, despite the expense of more extravagant gifts. The only element that will truly make a difference to the grandchildren is the time you spend with them. This, however, is no competition. It's a joy!

Daughters and Sons

Oh, my son's my son 'til he gets him a wife,
but my daughter's my daughter all her life.
—D. Craik

If your daughter has a child you are lucky, indeed. Regardless of your previous relationship, a door has opened between you. Now, she can understand where you are coming from—or at least where you started. Now, you are the undeniable expert. It's the ideal opportunity to become friends. Mothers and daughters classically have their highs and lows. My mother and I were no exception. Everything's changed now. Not only do we have motherhood in common, but also we both want the best for my children.

Shower that baby with all the love and affection that you have to offer. Don't wait for your daughter's invitation for anything—except advice. Just because you decked her out in fancy little dresses doesn't mean they are appropriate for your grandchild—even baby fashions change. Keep your relationship alive by being clear with each other about visiting hours. The rest is easy.

No one can resist another person who loves their baby. Your daughter will be able to see you from a whole new perspective. She will enjoy the view . . . and you will gain easy access to your grandchild.

Sons-In-Law

Fathers have become a luxury item in our society. If you have a son-in-law, especially one who lives with your grandchildren, count your blessings. He is very important to your grandchildren's well-being. If he is gone, you are likely to become his replacement. It's best for the children to have you both.

Make friends . . . it's easier than you think. Have you heard the joke about how some men marry their mother? It's not just a laughing matter. It works the other way, as well. Some women unconsciously seek men who have qualities in common with their mother. Either way, you have common ground. If your daughter is like you in any respect, then he will automatically relate to that part of you. If she is like his mother, then you must be a bit like his mother, as well.

If you can't put your finger on anything remotely similar between the three of you, relax. Perhaps you are relatively close in age and have some history in common. Perhaps you share a bit of geography. It could be that you have a mutual interest in some hobby.

In my family, both my husband and my mother are well read. They are also well versed in movie trivia. She prefers romances to his Westerns, but it makes no difference. My husband doesn't really care who is the director's daughter by whom or by which marriage, but he almost always knows. My mother sometimes calls him up to verify her stories or to point out something about an old movie that's appearing on television. The other day, she called to discuss the original filming of "Silas Marner." She thought she'd surprise him with some new information, but he knew even more than she did. They connect. If there's a trivia game nearby, watch out. My husband won't get involved, but when my mother gets stuck (a rare event), he'll look up from the paper and give it a shot.

The least common denominator in your relationship with your son-in-law is also the greatest: the grandchildren. No matter what aggravation may arise between you, the relationship will forge ahead because you are both crazy about the children. If your son-in-law happens to be one of those unusual fathers who have trouble relating, or truly appreciating young children, you can help. Get him involved by asking where those cute ears came from. Request a viewing of his baby pictures. It's always safe to ask a man about himself—it's the closest thing to outright flattery. You can't make it any easier than when you compare the baby's spunky character or twinkling eyes to the father's.

You don't have to be equals to be friends with your son-in-law. In fact, you really can't be pals on that level. You are the superior being. You did give birth to the woman he loves, after all. Without you, his little bundle of joy wouldn't be here. Give your son-in-law the chance to treat you with respect. Let him know how you expect to be treated by acting in a manner that deserves respect.

Let your presence in your son-in-law's life be a positive one. Send him birthday cards. Have one of his favorite foods on hand when he visits. (My mother usually stocks up on pistachio ice cream.) Be patient. Your daughter can help, but only you can make it work.

Daughters-In-Law

She wants to love you! She may not know it, but loving you would make her life so much easier—and a lot more fun. As the grandmother, you have a lot of power. Use it to empower your daughter-in-law. She will be grateful and you will end up where you started off—powerful. You've simply put everything in a positive light.

Your goal is to be the consummate grandmother. Never lose sight of this objective. It relies a great deal on your relationship with this woman. You don't have to be crazy about your daughter-in-law, but give her the benefit of the doubt. Watch her with your son and your grandchild. You might really learn to like her a lot.

My friend, Eileen, never felt close to her daughter-in-law. Jill was a modern young wife, open in her concern about how a child would interfere with her busy career and social life. Their relationship could best be described as reserved—and reserved for holidays. For several years, it didn't seem to matter. Since the baby was born, however, the two women have realized that they are more alike than different. More than anything else, they love the same man and his baby. They are working partners in their family's life.

The easiest way to get your daughter-in-law to like you is to let her know you are on her team. If you can, take her to lunch while she's pregnant or for her first time out with the baby. Tell her you are on her side—then follow through. Help make life easier for her.

Let your daughter-in-law set the pace. If she doesn't know you very well, let her see how you respond to her beloved baby. Show her how much you love that little tike. Even if you raised four children, ask her opinion about which baby bonnet she would prefer you to buy. Bring her a frozen casserole so she doesn't have to cook. Offer to watch the baby while she takes a nap or gets her hair cut. Rent a video or take a class in CPR to assure her that you care enough to be a safe baby-sitter. Most importantly, let her know that you would love to help, within reason.

If she doesn't want your assistance, give her some space. Offer it for another time. Her reserved demeanor doesn't mean she's a snob or she doesn't like you. It probably means she is shy or nervous about not knowing how to please you. Maybe she imagines that you are hovering close, watching to see if she's a good mother. That's enough to make anyone insecure, self-conscious and clumsy. Who knows what her husband told her about you? Possibly very little. Tell her about yourself. Tell her about your son and what it was like being his Mommy. Describe what her baby's father was like as a baby. It's a sure icebreaker.

Since you value this relationship, it's easy to be taken advantage of. If things get out of hand, gently tell her you're not available. Set limits. You'll both be much happier if you know exactly where you stand. Let it be a two-way street. Encourage your daughter-in-law to kick you out when you've overstayed your welcome. Phrase it in a way that seems polite: ask her to let you know when she wants some privacy.

If you are there, and notice that she's getting irritable, suggest that you should be going. Make up some errand. If she is reluctant, maybe what she really needs is a ten-minute nap. If she doesn't respond, skedaddle. Wouldn't you rather be gone than resented? That baby has a lot of birthdays coming up—you want to be invited!

You know you're a member of Club Grandma when . . .

— you want to move next door to your daughter.
— your old clothes are back in style.
— you'll do anything to stop your grand-child's tears.
— everything the children do is wonderful, brilliant or adorable.
— you know about the new "Barney" mer-chandise before your local toy store does.

14.

⚜ ⚜ ⚜ ⚜ ⚜ ⚜

Family Challenge

God could not be everywhere so he created parents
and when they became too busy he created grandparents.
—Sunie Levin, author

Divorce

The "D" word is everywhere. You can try to explain the infinite advantages of commitment and the immeasurable tragedies of divorce. You can offer your own experience as an example. You can even suggest counseling. Once you've contributed this sage advice, step back and stay out of it.

Should this marriage be worked out? Should it be ended? It affects you, your child and your grandchildren. It is entirely your business . . . yet it is none of your business. Even though it is public, it is deeply personal—and you are not that person. Resist the temptation. Be supportive, but do not get involved. There is too much private history you don't know and too many intimate details that you will never learn. Logic rarely prevails over emotions. Your interference will make you an enemy in both camps.

Worst of all, divorce can make it difficult to sustain a close relationship with your grandchildren. Don't give up! Those kids need you now more than ever. Regardless of how many friends' parents are divorced or how well they seem to be taking it, the pain is there and it will manifest itself someday.

Today's young adults are the first generation that are as likely to have been raised in broken homes as not. Divorce is so prevalent that even the term "broken home" seems antiquated. "Dysfunctional family" is a term that is liberally applied, yet rarely linked with responsibility. According to current cultural theories, we are all "victims." Just because divorce is common, however, doesn't mean it should be condoned. We have to think about the children.

During a recent visit, Juliette told me a story about how her friend Elizabeth's father is marrying a woman who is not Elizabeth's mother. She wanted to know if her father and mother are getting married again. She also mentioned that Jason was visiting his father over the weekend. Today, she watched "Barney" then explained to me how families come in all shapes and kinds. She recognized that this is true and she was comfortable with the idea. Yet, when I asked her how she felt about that, she thought for a moment and said that the children will be sad without their Mommy and their Daddy at home.

Here are the golden rules:

1. *Be brave.* You are part of the happy picture. Stay in the picture even when things are, shall we say, tense. Focus on the children and ignore the rest. Keep as much of the happy part alive as possible. The show must go on. Life does.

2. *Have boundaries.* Your relationship with your grandchildren is separate from their relationship with their parents. Be consistent in your habits with the children. Do not take sides—at least not out loud. Anything negative that you say about either parent will hurt the child. Even if it is a known fact that one parent committed adultery, and the child is a teenager, old enough to understand, it will hurt. It will hurt if it is a mean accusation and it will hurt even more if it is the truth. To a child, it is a kind of betrayal. Don't rub it in.

Especially omit comparisons of the parents. Your grandchild needs to love both parents and have a continuing relationship with each one. They must live with this for the rest of their lives. Accentuate the positive . . . you.

3. *Avoid triangles.* Focus your stories on yourself. Your longing for a different outcome will only add to your grandchild's anxiety. The adjustment is difficult. Don't dig for information or plan miracle cures. Your grandchild needs you to lean on. Create a warm, wonderful world where you take over and no one has to deal with the ugly realities of divorce. Take advantage of this time to bring them into your world. Let them get to know you—it will be a distraction that will leave you with an even closer relationship.

Custody

A Grandma Is Forever

During the process of separation and divorce, volunteer to join the couple in a child-oriented counseling session with a family therapist. Ask how you can help during this period of transition. Plan a visit around this important event in your family's life. If you cannot, feel free to contact a local family therapist and explore these issues on your own. Focus on how you can be involved with the children in a positive manner.

If you are on good terms with both parents, have a talk with the one getting custody about your future with the children. If your child will not get custody, take the spouse to lunch or have a heart-to-heart on the telephone about your wish to remain in the child's life. Stress how much you love your grandchildren and how important that is for them. If you are not on wonderful terms with the spouse, request that you be included in the custody agreement with reference to visitation rights that are in "the best interest of" the children. If necessary, call both attorneys directly to discuss this important matter. Try not to get roped into exact schedules—you are more likely to enjoy a fuller relationship with the children on a more relaxed and impulsive timetable. It pays to plan ahead. Don't assume you will be free to see them.

Until Death Do You Part: Remarriage

No matter who wins custody, you cannot lose. The grandchildren are yours. Another wedding doesn't change this a bit—it just blesses the children with additional grandparents. They deserve all the love they can get. If you are the grandma on the outside, don't forget those children are your blood and you have every right to see them. Help the children feel comfortable in the new situation by being a consistent presence. Don't reject them if your child loses custody and "strangers" now raise them. They will feel abandoned by you. Who is being punished here? The children are innocent. So are you.

It's overwhelming when a parent remarries. Often it means a new house, a new school and new siblings. New grandparents could tip the bucket. If you have just become the proud new grandparent of your child's new stepchildren, be sensitive to normal feelings of denial that you are, in fact, their grandparent. Be gentle. Treat them the same as your grandchildren. Odds are, you'll have time alone with the original ones when the new ones go visit their other grandparents.

Draw the children into your traditional activities and create new ones that involve them—whether it's playing checkers or videotaping T-ball practice. If there are problems, speak to their parents about it. Eventually, the children will settle into a comfortable relationship with you. Then they'll agree that when it comes to grandparents, the more, the merrier.

Don't be afraid of the new step-parent. Your grandchildren are likely to be scared enough for everyone. Your respect for a new step-parent will allow him or her to appreciate you. After all, you are helping them out by spending time with the children and making them happy.

Visiting Hours

If possible, see the children away from the custodial parent's influence. Even if your son or daughter has custody, let them know that you are not just part of that package. You are a big part of their heritage, all by yourself. Take them out. Invite them to visit your home, even if it means that you must pick them up and bring them there.

If your son or daughter does not have custody, there is no reason why he or she must share their sacred visitation period with you. Have your own special time. You both deserve it.

Single Parents

When your child is raising your grandchildren single-handedly, your role is even more vital. As four out of five grandmothers say, "You can catch more flies with honey than with vinegar." This holds true even when dealing with family. After all, it's their turf you are stepping on. There may be plenty of pitfalls in his or her methods. Try not to be critical or judgmental. Instead, join in and help.

Your Daughter

Studies show that a strong grandmother can serve as a substitute for an absent father. It is true that single women can raise children to be productive and responsible members of society. There are reasons, however, that it takes two to procreate. Mainly, it is a lot easier. There is half as much pressure and twice as much energy. This is where you fit in. You can be more than a lifesaver—you can be a fairy God-mother! Plus, you have all your experience and wisdom to offer.

The only difference between interference and help is an invitation. Ask how you can help and if you can make some suggestions.

Try the approach I suggest in therapy: frame your inquiries with "I" statements. Instead of "you're doing that all wrong," try "I know a way that might be easier . . ." Instead of "you should let me do that," try "I'd really enjoy doing that." It helps put things in a more gentle, positive approach without making any undue assumptions or accusations toward the other person. Actually, it is a useful tool in everyday communication. It is an ideal way for people to work together without stepping on each other's toes.

Your Son

If your son is the sole parent, you can be a surrogate Mom. Of course, everything is easier if you live nearby. Then you can help with the traditional chores of cooking, shopping, and so forth. Your real value, however, is far more important. While a housekeeper can provide feminine support, her love is not guaranteed. Children need your nurturing. Even if Daddy's girlfriend is playing "Mommy," the children need consistent emotional support.

It's as if you are a security blanket—a perfectly soft, warm cotton blanket that your grandchildren snuggle in. Cashmere would be softer and wool would be warmer, but it's no fun when they get yanked away without warning. You are the blanket that will always be soft and will always be warm and will always be there. You can even be a security blanket for your son.

You know you're a member of Club Grandma when . . .

— you give holiday gifts months before the holidays.
— you keep a box in your closet for forgotten toys.
— you don't mind being spit up on.
— you buy a piñata.

The Vote's are In !

15.
Club Poll

Only a mother knows a mother's fondness.
—Lady Montague, 1754

Aquestionnaire was offered randomly to families around the country. Respondents of the survey were religiously diverse and ranged from lower middle class to upper class. Questions were addressed both to the parents and to the grandmothers.

The parents were scattered around the country, with a majority residing in California. Most of these parents were not raised on the West coast: the grandmothers lived in Florida, New Jersey, Ohio and many states in between. Some had moved to be closer to their grandchildren.

The mothers tended to be in their late twenties or their thirties, with children ranging from one month to ten years old. The number of grandchildren ranged from one to ten, with the majority numbering four.

The most consistent response came not from a question on the poll, but rather from the poll itself: the grandmothers were unanimously eager to talk about their grandchildren. The parents felt it was a good excuse to speak with their folks. All things are not equal, however, and 95 percent of the parents responding to the poll were mothers.

1. **Mom's mother is . . . nearby** _____ **far away** _____
   Dad's mother is . . . nearby _____ **far away** _____

Sixty-five percent of maternal grandmothers lived nearby.
Ten percent of paternal grandmothers lived nearby.
Coincidence?

2. She is . . . a lot of help _____ a nuisance _____ other _____

Maternal grandmothers were helpful; paternal grandmothers were generally "other"—not around much, but helpful when they were. These answers lent credence to the results of the question regarding proximity. However, they bring up a chicken or egg dilemma: are the maternal grandmothers helpful because they are close, or are they close because they are helpful?

3. Your favorite thing about grandma is:

Maternal grandmothers were lauded for their emotional involvement: the love and adoration of the children. Parents were also grateful for having someone there when they needed them.

Praise for paternal grandmothers was more objective about the women themselves: they were "bright" with "common sense", they "knew the place," they were willing to help with almost anything, especially weaning babies to the bottle (they preferred the bottle). Several were praised for being the stereotypical grandma who sewed, made dolls and quilts and baked with the children. The most personal praise was for women who were thoughtful and supportive of the mother's maternal desires.

4. Your least favorite thing about grandma is:

The number one complaint about grandmothers was that they live too far away. After that, the answers were evenly split between those mothers who received too much criticism and unwanted advice and those who wanted more "insight based on past experiences" and more understanding and "knowledge about what kids do at various developmental stages." Other responses mentioned small town narrow-mindedness, wishy-washiness and an "aversion to changing diapers."

5. Since having kids, has your relationship with grandma changed? How?

All mothers felt that their relationship with their own mother had improved since the grandchildren was born. Most felt they had finally earned respect as an adult. They also had more in common. Some felt it was better because the focus was no longer on them—it was now on the grandchildren. The mother's relationship with their mother-in-laws, for the most part, did not change. Some felt things were better. The greatest change was that, good or bad, grandchildren forced them to interact more.

6. What suggestions would you give to grandma if you could?

Mothers were all over the map with suggestions for the grandmothers. More than a few requested unconditional love. Many wanted grandma to recognize that "kids are smart, so treat them that way." There were great many requests for an end to unwanted advice—including "recipes for homemade baby food." More than a few wanted to reassure grandma that their granddaughter was not fat—she was only six months old! There was also a group of mothers who were nervous about the length of time between motherhood and grandmotherhood and wished that grandma would learn infant CPR and review emergency procedures so they would feel more comfortable having her baby-sit.

Suggestions for paternal grandmothers were far more consistent. The first word in 60 percent of the responses was "relax." Mothers went on to reassure grandmas that the kids "love you and remember you even though they don't see you much." Many reminded that a baby's crying is no reflection on grandma. Others asked that grandma concentrate on enjoying the children rather than giving their folks grief.

Finally, it was grandma's turn. . . .

1. What's the best part of being a grandma?

27%   The joy of loving the children.

27%   Watching the children grow and develop their own personalities.

18%   All the fun without all the responsibility—"when the baby starts crying you can go home."

9%   Being loved by them—"getting return smiles that melt my heart."

9%   Interacting with the children.

9%   The extended family—"full and joyful holidays."

2. What's the worst part of being a grandma?

Eighty-one percent of respondents were emphatic that living far away or not seeing the grandchildren often enough was the worst part. The other 19 percent felt there was nothing bad about being a grandparent.

3. Do you visit . . . anytime _____ call first _____ plan ahead _____

Eighty-one percent planned ahead for visits, most likely because they lived far away. Ten percent called first and 9 percent visited anytime.

4. What are your favorite activities to do with your grand-children?

36%   Talking—interacting, making them laugh.

36%   Taking walks, preferably one child at a time (which provides the opportunity to talk)

20%   Cuddling and hugging.

8% An assortment of activities including playing on the floor, swimming, biking, teaching new things, going to the playground and going on vacation to enjoy all these things.

5. What do you do differently now that you're a grandma?

The following answers were equally popular . . .

1. knit
2. baby-sit
3. buy more presents
4. watch them instead of trying to get anything done
5. make plans with them in mind
6. think of them constantly—"they're #1 in my life"
7. "identify more with *my* daughter"
8. think more of the future
9. shop for baby food

6. What advice would you give to a new grandma?

The same two answers popped up over and over . . .

1. Relax and enjoy every minute of it—"it's the most fabulous thing in the world."
2. Don't interfere: "don't try to be a mother again," "cool it."

Others answers included reminders to not forget about sons and daughters—they need love and attention, too.

7. What surprised you most about being a grandma?

Twenty-seven percent were most surprised at their intense feelings of love for their grandchildren.

Other answers were about equal, including . . .

1. everything
2. nothing
3. the fact that they didn't have to be "old with grey hair in a bun" to be a grandma
4. difference in stamina
5. all the grandchildren were "beautiful and outstanding"
6. "how wonderful it is"
7. didn't think they were ready until it happened

8. Has your relationship changed with your daughter/son-in-law?

60% Said yes: there was more understanding and more respect for their daughter-in-law's opinions, the sons-in-laws inspire more confidence plus admiration for their fatherly pride. Recognizing parts of the parents in the children makes it easier on both sides.

40% Said there is no change: this answer emerged from the extremes of either having a great relationship already or not having much of a relationship at all.

9. What's the funniest thing that's happened to you as a grandma?

Most of the answers described the kind of situations where "you had to be there" to appreciate them. There were "pearls of wisdom" from three-year-olds, funny nicknames, brute honesty about nose hair and a request for the backyard when the grandparents "expire." Many grandmas were amazed at how everything about birthing and childcare has changed since they were mothers.

Club Poll

• • • • •

This poll was by no means scientific; nevertheless, the results were consistent and reliable in terms of the average grandmother.

The most interesting result is the coincidence between the mothers' suggestions for grandmothers versus the grandmothers' suggestions for other grandmothers. The mothers asked the grandmothers to relax and enjoy the children and to stop interfering with unwanted advice. The grandmothers, without knowing about the preceding answers, suggested the very same things.

This indicates one of two things: either grandmothers are not listening to themselves, or they are consciously trying to stop interfering. In some cases, grandmothers allowed that this is "difficult." Indeed, it takes a delicate balance to walk the fine line of offering advice. If you help too much, you can be interfering. If you don't help, you aren't interfering, but you aren't helping either. Damned if you do, damned if you don't. You might as well err on the side of the children.

The poll's most conclusive result is that everyone agrees grandmas aren't around enough. Take heed.

You know you're a member of Club Grandma when . . .

— you ride the roller coaster for the first time in twenty-five years.
— you buy a new camera.
— you start baking again.
— Father's Day is at the kids' house.

16.

Out-of-Town Members

No one . . . who has not known that inestimable privilege
can possibly realize what good fortune it is
to grow up in a home where there are grandparents.
—Suzanne Lafollette, writer (1893–1983)

The biggest complaint about grandmas is that you live too far away! The only advantage is that you might not worry so much: you know everyone has to solve their own problems. However, if one of those problems is that you're too far away, here are some things to keep in mind. . . .

Common Concerns

1. *Invitations.* Don't wait for an invitation! It could be a long wait. It's not that they don't want to have you, it's just that there is rarely a perfect time for a visit. Ask your daughter or son—and especially their spouse—when would be a good time to visit. Give them some concrete dates to choose from. That way, you all make a commitment and it *will* happen.

2. *The "Big Event."* My mother's friend, Louise, is always talking about her grandchildren. She lives in Ohio; they live in Montana. She can't wait to see them, but it's not exactly right around the corner. They always invite her during the course of conversation, but she isn't sure if they are sincere or just being polite. Since she isn't used to visiting them, she feels like she would be intruding to force herself on them without a good excuse. So, she is waiting for a big event, like graduation.

Personally, I think she's holding out until a talk show host takes pity on her and reunites the family on network television!

Don't wait. It doesn't have to be Christmas or Hanukkah or a family reunion. If families saw each other more often, reunions wouldn't be such a big deal, anyway. If you visit during an ordinary part of the year, you'll learn the routine. You'll become familiar with where the dentist, the dance class, and the grocery store are—you may even get to know some neighbors. On the next visit, things will feel much cozier for everyone and you can be relaxed as well as more helpful. Don't wait for a big event. You *are* the big event.

3. *Bad blood.* If strained relations are keeping you from seeing the grandchildren, rise above it. You love those children despite their parents' bad graces. There is no relationship between the two. Why should the children miss out? Don't let pride get in the way of those sweet kisses. It's not necessary to make up—some issues may never be resolved. Simply put it behind you. If a disagreement is keeping you from your grandchildren, then you are losing. Love is waiting in your grandchildren's hearts with your name on it. It's yours, you deserve it—go get it!

4. *Continuity.* Remember back in grade school, when a week seemed like a million years? Imagine what six months must feel like. See your grandchildren as often as you can. Strangers at the grocery store are constantly telling me to enjoy the children while they are babies, because it goes by so quickly. I smile and nod and thank them, then shake my head and head for the diaper aisle. I only notice the time passing when I develop a roll of film that was lost in my purse for a few weeks—the changes are startling.

You want to know the children, not just remember them as babies. You don't want to be remembered by what you gave

132

them for their birthday and if the card was late or inappropri-ate. Photographs are wonderful, but your scrapbook will be a lot more fun if the pictures of your grandchildren include you.

The Visit

1. *How long is too long?* Since the travel time is great, you are likely to stay awhile. Two weeks is plenty. If you are sleeping on the couch, one week is even better. If there is a guest room or you are staying elsewhere, go for two. Even if you are on great terms with everybody, having a house guest is a lot of work. It's also very stressful. (Even good things create stress.) When the guest is somebody's mother, that goes double.

2. *Make a plan.* Let your family know the date you are leaving before you arrive. This will frame the visit as a controlled event. When you arrive, sit down with everyone to discuss your plans. (Do the same thing when they visit you.) Build some structure into the visit by defining the things that you really want to do. Without structure, there is chaos. On the other hand, too much structure is no fun. Your daughter or son may have tickets for you to visit Hearst Castle or see the new play. Perhaps they have reserved a rental car for you. Commit to what you would like to do with them or without them.

Be assertive about the type of visit you prefer. Do you want to relax like a real vacation or do you want to get involved and be helpful? If you do want to help, let them know how. Explain that you don't feel safe driving with the children, so you won't want to drive car pools, but you would enjoy making dinner Wednesday night and taking everyone to brunch on Sunday . . . or whatever it is that you prefer. Maybe you'd like to help by getting the adults a glass of wine before dinner. Maybe it would be fun to give the baby her bath or shop with the ten-year-old for new shoes. Allow for choices.

My friend, Lydia, complained that her mother-in-law did the dishes Sunday night. I couldn't understand why this was a problem. Lydia explained to me that she does the dishes every night, while her husband is only responsible for Sunday. Her mother-in-law wasn't helping her at all, she was just letting her son get out of his share of the work. So, be careful not to step on toes, even when you are helping. Be supportive of the one who's doing all the work.

3. *Pace yourself.* My mother goes gangbusters when we are together. She is fully capable of doing every activity with the kids for forty-eight hours. Then she can't move for three days. Remember, kids are accepting. They'll be just as happy lying on the couch with you, reading or watching cartoons, as long as you are together.

4. *Real life.* Let the children keep to their routines. Experience your grandchildren's life with them. Accompany them to their activities, unless it is embarrassing for them. No offense personally, but teenagers will appreciate it if you let them decide where you take them. Bowling might be off limits; gymnastics might be fun. On your own turf, and as an adult, you automatically make this choice. Treat them with the same respect. This is their turf.

5. *Be yourself.* No matter who is visiting whom, don't try too hard to impress them. You want to get to know your real grandchildren; let them get to know the real you!

Extenuating Circumstances

If you cannot visit them and they cannot visit you, all is not lost. Plenty of people in nursing homes or without funds to travel cross country enjoy good relationships with their grand-children. How? By taking advantage of other means of communication.

Telephone Time

It's true that people tend to be more intimate on the telephone than in person. There are no eyes to judge you and no distractions. Call your long-distance phone company to find a frequent calling plan that will include your grandchildren's area. Or, set up a regular Sunday evening phone date.

Teenagers love to talk on the telephone—especially if you talk about them. Ask about their boyfriends and their favorite new clothing style. Ask their opinion on movies and gun control and the President's latest veto. They'll appreciate someone who cares about what they think. Eventually, they are bound to get curious and ask about you.

Children love to talk on the telephone, too. Inquire about their friends and hobbies and what they had for dinner. Volunteer information about your day. Make up funny food combinations that you had for dinner, like octopus and cotton candy, and they'll go wild. Tell them stories about how you rode on a giant singing caterpillar with red fur and purple polka dots. If you're worried about how impressionable they are and fear that you might be contributing to potential nightmares, confess that you're just being silly. They'll love you for it.

Pen Pals

Write letters that include stamped postcards for your grand-children to send back to you. With any luck, they'll jot down a

135

few words before they mail them. Younger children will feel important when they get your mail and they will enjoy writing important letters back. Older children might not show it, but they'll enjoy the attention, too. Use Elvis stamps or something else fun and significant. If you ask your grandchildren for specific information, like what times they got in the swim meet this week, and keep sending stamped returned envelopes, they are bound get the hint. (If not, feel free to write a hint in capital letters.) Writing is a lost skill. With a little perseverance, you can bring it back.

Seeing Is Believing

If you have a videotape recorder, you can send your grand-children home movie messages. Ask a friend to be your camera operator. Or set up the camera somewhere, wave your arms and talk a lot. Or you could videotape a walking tour while you talk, then hold out the camera, turn it around and give them a kiss good-bye.

Letters by Ear

Audio tapes can be even more fun, because they are less threatening. It's not such a big deal. You won't be tempted to brush your hair or clean the room for your tape recorder. Just press "record" and start talking. Keep a running list of entertaining topics right next to your grocery list.

Younger children will love hearing your voice, no matter what you are saying. Teenagers will think it's cool and listen to you while they procrastinate studying. Or they can play your tape in the car when there are too many commercials on the radio.

A tape can be heard by anyone, regardless of who it is intended for, so your grandchild might enjoy hiding out or listening in privacy with headphones. In fact, inexpensive headphones would make a good birthday gift. Encourage your grandchild to record his response and any additional ramblings right over your message on the same tape. You can use cardboard audio tape mailers and label them "top secret" or "for your ears only" to make them a really big deal.

Keep in touch!

You know you're a member of Club Grandma when . . .

— you buy film in multi-packs.
— your children start listening to your opinions.
— you reschedule all your appointments around your grandchildren's visit.
— you know who Baby Bop is.

17.
⬦ ⬦ ⬦ ⬦ ⬦ ⬦ ⬦ ⬦
Club Events

My Grandma just got arrested on TV, you wanna know why?
My Grandmother loves us so much that she's gone to jail to save us
from the bomb.
—Edward, age 5

Activity Roster

One of the best parts of being a grandmother is connecting with others outside of your family. Not only do you have something in common with trillions of other proud women, but your status as a grandmother can enhance your relationships with everyone else. After all, everyone has a grandmother, whether on Earth or in Heaven.

If your grandchildren are too far away to play with on a regular basis, you can get involved with other children who are nearby. Here are some activities you might enjoy.

- With a giant bubble wand and a bucket of dish soap you could be the "Bubble Lady" at the park. Children love bubbles. Parents might look at you funny at first, but once they know you're a grandma, they'll look forward to seeing you.
- Hospitals and orphanages will welcome your attention. Call the administrator for permission to read stories to individual children or a group. Many children would appreciate a grandma to talk to, even without a book.

138

- Check with the library about a Grandparents Reading to Children program. Our local library has one every afternoon from 2:00 to 4:00. Stories are always popular with children—and they contribute to a greater appreciation of reading. Story time also gives parents and caregivers some time to relax and read books without pictures. Reading programs can be informal, where the children pick the books or they can be planned programs that include a related craft activity. One round, tike-sized table in the children's area and a free hour or two every week is all that you need to begin. With prior arrangements, any library would love to have you.
- Public schools can always use volunteers to distribute milk or help on the playground. Many under-budgeted school districts need volunteers to give art and music classes. You don't need a degree or expertise—just enthusiasm about the subject.
- Call the local Girl Scout Council to inquire about being a helper for troop meetings.
- A Parks and Recreation organization could refer you to a soccer league that is in need of another coach.

If you live close to your grandchild, there are many ways to be involved in their lives. You may enjoy participating in school or recreational programs:

- Volunteer to be Room Grandma. There are never enough Room Parents at school, and with so many parents working, you'll be doubly appreciated.
- Join the Parents Association and get involved with the lunch program or whatever else interests you.

- Help with the class party on your favorite holiday.
- Supervise or carpool during a school field trip.
- Give a special presentation that the students would be interested in. Ask the teacher for suggestions. Depending on the age, you could help kids make peanut butter and jelly sandwiches, an egg carton caterpillar, or a mural.
- Help staff a bake sale.
- Have a Grandma booth at the school carnival and charge a nickel per hug!

Being involved with children can be joyous for you as well as the children. Even if you've been a social doyenne all your life, raising money for charities and good causes, there is something different about offering your time as a Grandmother. The difference is love.

Political Rallies

Have you voted since you became a grandmother? If so, I'll bet you thought twice about that school bond issue on the ballot. Maybe you've even started recycling. Rather than burrowing in as your life winds through familiar territory, now is the perfect opportunity to look up and be a part of the world at large. You have a valuable perspective on the world's potential. And goodness knows, you have real live, huggable reasons to care about what happens in the next month, the next year, and the next century. Your young grandchildren can't vote yet, but you can make sure their interests are represented.

Have you ever seen a grandmother arrested for political activism? How many grandmas lead influential delegations at party conventions? When is the last time you saw a grandmother collecting signatures outside the post office? You would remember, right? Grandmas stand out in every political crowd. The public sympathizes with grandmas, because you represent everything good and loving about families. Consequently, your support of any issue or candidate is quite influential. You don't have to get arrested, but your efforts on the local level of your favorite cause can make a big difference. Your opinion counts—a lot.

Grandmothers For Peace, an international organization based in Elk Grove, California, began in a grandma's living room in 1982 and now holds conferences around the world. Communication between grandmothers of many nations are providing help on a personal scale as well as echoing in the halls of parliament. Join a local chapter of a group that interests you—or start a new one—to address your concerns about the world your grandchildren are inheriting.

Grandmas can make a difference. The future is yours.

Pep Rallies

Last week a little girl ran up behind a woman at the grocery store. Excited, she called, "Hi Grandma!" The woman froze in her tracks, turned around and offered a benign smile. Obviously, the prospect did not thrill her. The girl's mother rushed up to claim her, apologetic. The woman turned on her heel so quickly that the mother's embarrassment turned quickly to disdain. She called after the woman, "She loves her Grandma!"

Several days later, a teenager pulled his battered van up behind an older woman at the gas pump. The woman was in control of the Self Serve pump, yet she worked at her own pace. The boy climbed out of his car, paid at the cashier booth and returned to find the woman slowly screwing her gas cap back on. He glanced at his watch and said, "In this lifetime, Grandma!" The woman pulled her shoulders back and turned to him. A proud smile spread across her face. "Why, thank-you, son!"

Being a grandmother isn't about being old, or even passing the torch to younger generations. It's about being loved and revered. It's an existential role in a transient world. Every time you hear the noble title, think of it as a cheer. Hip hip hooray! Be proud.

Class Reunions

When people unite after a long time, peer pressure returns in the form of jealousy and competition. Beauty, wealth and prestige are important, but they are not everything.

Recently my mother traveled across the country to her high school reunion in New Jersey. Here is Nana's story:

An old beau approached me with his new wife. The wife was younger, of course, and he was working on his second family. He eyed me carefully and complemented my youth and vitality. I smiled at the wife and reminded him that I'm still younger than he is. He hugged his wife closer. I pulled out my trump card and showed him pictures of my grandchildren. He dropped his embrace to hold the photographs. "Oh, you're so lucky. I don't have any grandchildren yet."

After the fete for our older daughter's first birthday, we decided to think small for the second. We put the burden on Nana, who accepted it gladly, and held a picnic in the park near her house. The only guests, outside of family, were two friends of my mother's. When they had enough of diapers and birthday cake, they decided to leave. They walked toward their cars and waved good-bye. Unbidden, the baby waved back and blew kisses. Nana, bursting with pride, turned to me and declared, "Now, that's status!"

You know you're a member of Club Grandma when . . .

—your birthday book is always open.
—you buy colored popcorn.
—you look forward to Halloween.
—you send Mother's Day cards to your daughter.

18.

. . . .

Membership Profile

Who takes a child by the hand
takes the mother by the heart.
—Danish proverb

Picture Marlene Dietrich on the cover of *Life* magazine in August, 1948. A sultry siren, the ultimate femme fatale . . . would you believe "Grandmother Dietrich"? That's what they called her, and so she was. Having grandchildren enhanced her version of the older, sexual female. It added classic beauty to the Grandma Hall of Fame. In fact, Ms. Dietrich disguised herself in a nurse uniform to stroll her grandson through Central Park. She bought her daughter a brownstone and lived in a Park Avenue hotel until she found a suitable home nearby. In interviews, she explained that she worked to take care of her family. A woman extraordinaire? No, just your average, everyday Grandma.

What do you, Barbara Bush, Whoopi Goldberg, Priscilla Presley, and Raquel Welch have in common? You guessed it: grandchildren! Which proves that grandmothers come in every size, color, style and shape. As long as your arms fit around the baby, you are perfect.

Single Grandmas

Men die younger than women. It's a fact. It follows that there are quite a few single grandmas out there. Divorce multiplies the situation. As Nana will attest, grandchildren go a long way to fill up a single grandma's heart.

If you have a boyfriend, that's terrific. Don't let him come between you and your grandchildren. You might both enjoy visiting your grandchildren separately. If you want to bring him along on your visits or include him at your place, fine. Just be sure to focus your attention on the kids. They're the "sure thing"!

Step-Grandmas

If you are a new step-Grandma, dive right in. More people to love equals more people to love you back. Try not to have any expectations—you may not be welcomed with tiny open arms. Accept that the children might be nervous with you. Just remember, the way to a man's heart isn't only through his stomach! If you initiate a real relationship with his grandchildren, everyone will benefit. If you can't stand the kids, be comforted that you had nothing to do with them getting that way. You *can* have something to do with making them nicer.

If you have married a widower, you are desperately needed to fulfill the grandma role, whether the children consciously realize this or not. If you married a divorcee, you can help him maintain or re-establish a good relationship with his grandchildren. In every case, be consistent. When you accept the responsibilities of being a grandma, all the benefits will be yours as well.

My step-grandmother came into my life when my real grandma was alive and flourishing, so we naturally called our grandfather's wife by her first name. Twenty years later, my hand hesitates each time I write that name on a letter to her and my grandfather. She's always been supportive, loving, generous—and a real kick to be around. She has always made an effort to connect with me by spending time alone with me or with my family and she has succeeded. She never tried to replace my grandma; she is unique in her own way. She is truly a grandma.

"Step" doesn't have to be a four-letter word. You can bring joy to many lives, including your own.

Remarried Grandmas

It's okay to visit your grandchildren without your husband. Maybe it will work out that you each visit grandchildren at the same time. If you spend time with the grandchildren as a team, be sure you get equal time. If you were single for awhile, you may have had many impromptu visits. That's less likely to happen now, so plan ahead. If your husband doesn't have grandchildren, don't let him keep you away. On the contrary, teach him how it's done. He'll learn to love it. Remember, your grandchildren will always be there for you as long as you are always there for them. Have an influence on the future—and a good time as well!

Adopted Grandmas

A grandma is a grandma is a grandma. Unconditional love takes patience and understanding. Contribute to the warm environment that will make your grandchild feel secure. Years from now, when the child has natural doubts about his adopted parents versus his genetic parents, your role in his life will not be questioned. You will always be Grandma.

Surrogate Moms

You may have finished raising your children, only to find yourself raising your children's children. This is not unusual. If you are the one who keeps track of when and what the children eat, then face it—you're the mother. With your wisdom and relaxed attitude about child rearing, the children are lucky to have you. Times do change, so it is important to keep up with current child development theories that may not have been proven when you raised your own children. Don't despair. Turn on the television to Dr. T. Berry Brazelton and Dr. Penelope Leach's parenting shows. Read the current books and magazines—you'll be amazed at how helpful they can be. Though your energy may flag, your great emotional expertise will serve you well. The children need you. They'll appreciate you more than you'll ever know. You may not be all fun and games, but you'll be one cherished grandma.

You know you're a member of Club Grandma when . . .

—you have popsicles in your freezer.
—you primp more for your grandchildren than you do for your husband.
—chicken pox don't make you nervous.
—when shopping, your feet automatically take you to the children's department.

19.
* * * * * * * *
Club History

What history our grandchildren carry within them.
If only D.N.A. could talk!
—Anonymous

In studies of vastly differing cultures by anthropologist Margaret Mead, grandmothers performed a major function. Remember those "National Geographic" films? The old women are wise and revered. The lower their breasts sag, the higher on the pedestal they go! Here is the natural order of things. Many animal kingdoms boast a matriarchal society as well. This natural order is based on those most responsible for the continuation of the species.

Although the grandmother/grandchild relationship is universal, outside change has also influenced families, particularly the rise of industrialization. Once families were pulled apart by factory work and the ease of transportation, both European and American societies came to value progress first and foremost. The grandmother, who maintained the humanistic values of the old culture, lost her place on the throne.

The immigrants who came to America embraced progress as the means to a successful future. Your grandmother may have grown up in a close-knit family with many generations living under one roof. When she became a mother, she held on to the ways of the Old World with such a fierce protectiveness that her children couldn't wait to break free. So, at the first scent of independence your mother escaped. When she had you, she gave you the gift of independence and few expectations of living in the same house, let alone the same city. When she retired, she may have moved even further away to the

148

sunbelt, Florida or Arizona. When you had children, she embraced modern grandparenting and established the twice a year visit. If she stayed for the summer, her friends called her bourgeois.

Today, the vast majority of grandparents have intermittent relationships. You've heard the debate over quality time versus quantity time in regard to career women? With grandparents there is nothing to argue about. The reality is that a good relationship with grandchildren is determined by the time you spend together. Whether it's weekly play dates or occasional visits backed up by telephone contact, the key word is "together."

Now it's your turn: you can have the best of both worlds. You don't have to stay in the background. Parents need you now! In this stressful world, it is an overwhelming task for parents to offer the bare necessities of financial security and role modeling. *Your* greatest purpose is to offer wisdom and love. For parents, children are the entree, for you, they are dessert!

You know you're a member of Club Grandma when . . .

— you smile when you lift up your couch cushion and find broken crayons and mashed cereal.
— children cry when you leave.
— your clothes are perfect for "dress-up."
— you stop to smell the roses.

20.

⊛ ⊛ ⊛ ⊛ ⊛ ⊛

Club Legacy

For finally, we are as we love.
It is love that measures our stature.
—William Sloane Coffin, Minister

What will your grandchildren remember when they grow up? What toys? What places? What events? What will they think of when they hear the word "grandmother"? Who was there when their parents were not? Who shared their secrets and dreams? What did they learn from you? What image of old age will guide them in later years? What kind of grandparents will *they* be?

Family History

What does it mean to be family? It means more than allergies and skin tone . . . more than attitudes and habits. It means a shared history, one that was influenced as much by outside influences as by heredity.

What were the places and people and politics that shaped you? Many cultures keep their history alive by telling stories around the campfire. This is how legends are made and how tall tales grow. Storytelling is also a way to bequeath your grandchildren a past that will send them confidently into the future.

Children love to hear stories about your childhood. They can relate to you more easily on their level. Identifying with you as a child will help them to feel especially close to you. Tell them everything you can remember about your family and relatives.

Photographs offer clear images for a child on which to base the visualization of your life. They also help to jog your memory and fill in wonderful details. In this transient world, it is important to give children a sense of belonging. A working knowledge of where they came from will help to create a healthy understanding of who they are.

Think of your brain as an Encyclopedia of Special Knowledge. Don't take all the insightful anecdotes and fascinating facts in your head along with you to Heaven. Tell your children and your grandchildren. Record your memories with a tape recorder, then pull out the "record" tab on the tape so it cannot be erased. Teach the children about the people they are descendants of and about the places that influenced them— and about you. This personal history is worth more than gold. It is all yours to give them.

Olden Times

Amaze your grandchildren with the wonders of progress. Tell them how you cooked popcorn without a microwave and watched movies without a VCR and listened to the radio before television. They will appreciate modern life.

Help them imagine running free in a daffodil covered field, walking down the street after dark and leaving the house without locking the door. They will appreciate "olden" times.

Traditions

Do you remember what you shared with your grandma? Can you share it with your grandchild? The most important tradition to uphold is that of being a loving grandparent.

When my first child was born, my mother took on the role of grandma with a vengeance. I figured it was partly the excitement of the new and that she would eventually settle back into her old routine with an extra bubble here and there. After all, she was raised in an untraditional family, with divorce before it was common. Today, she is the ultimate in grandmas, the grandma I wish on every child, and the one I hope to be. Since the day we began talking seriously about this book, tales of her own grandmother have come up frequently. And so it hit me. Her grandma was a good example of a grandma. It is likely that her grandma's grandma was also a "good" grandma . . . and hers before that. It is a pattern in the best sense of the word. Continue the tradition in your family . . . or start it with you.

I remember my grandma taking me to the duck pond. She was Irish, and I called her Nana—the same name my grandchildren call me. My Nana had long grey hair piled on her head. In the summer, she would visit and we would walk to the Jersey shore together. It was two blocks away and the duck pond was on the second block. Even today, I can describe the ducks and the swans and relive those days fifty years ago. Consequently, it is natural for me to take my granddaughter to a duck pond. My duck pond is a little different—a man-made canal in a condominium community. Nevertheless, there are still noisy ducks nesting on the grass, scurrying for every crumb of bread thrown to the water. Someday, I'll bet Juliette will take her grandchildren to feed the ducks. Who knows what a duck pond will look like by then. Who cares?

152

Traditions can be—OOPS! Sorry, my husband just burst in. It's 10:00 p.m. and he just got home from work, exhausted. Now he's all flushed with excitement, eyes shining like a young boy's. What happened? He opened the refrigerator and found the jar of old fashioned orange marmalade I picked up today at a specialty market. Evidently, it's the same brand his Nanny used to give him! Here I am, working on a chapter about traditions, and the sight of my husband's grandma's favorite orange marmalade has him conjuring up memories of those special times he shared with her. Obviously, traditions can be quite simple and still have a strong emotional effect.

Almost anything becomes special when it is a family tradition. Visiting Santa, getting a puppy for a birthday present, passing down an antique bracelet, getting a watch at graduation, even teaching a child to bowl can set off a pattern that is more beautiful to behold from a distance. Continue a family legacy—or create a new one.

Personal Connection

Did you ever keep a diary? Do you have any letters from friends that are so special you plan to keep them forever? How many times have you moved and discovered an old box full of treasures from days gone by? Each of these are personal connections to your past. The understanding you get reading about a difficult period of your life; the giggles that erupt at the sight of your first corsage; the warm glow in your heart as you read your friend's caring missive . . . these are all invaluable parts of your life. How about making a personal connection with your grandchild?

A friend of mine, Ralf, recently received a box of his late grandma's effects from Germany. Unfortunately, he never met his grandma. A bond existed, however, to the extent that he named his first child after her. This box was intended for the baby. When he opened it, he felt a more powerful connection to his grandma than he had ever imagined possible. Each item taught him about her and in turn, about himself. In essence, she has reached out from the past to take her place in the future. Her things will become symbols as well as part of the present for her namesake great grandchild.

Write a letter to your grandchildren. Whether or not you see them every week, pen an intimate note for each of them to peruse long after your visits are over. Explain what they mean to you, how you understand them now, and how you envision them to be in the future. Give them your innermost thoughts to savor, to cherish always. It will be more than a souvenir, it will be a part of their existence. Make that connection.

Everafter

Death is always traumatic, but a child's first experience with death will set the pace for all those to follow—including yours. Our ten-year-old cat died on Christmas Eve last year and it was torturous for all of us. We waited until after Christmas to tell our three-year-old, who adored him. There was so much excitement with Nana and Santa and all the gifts, that Juliette only asked about him once. We told her what had happened the next morning, and she has been talking about death ever since.

Almost every day, she asks another pragmatic question about Heaven. I realize that my answers will guide her beliefs for years to come, so I am a little nervous each time the topic arises. I act calm and try to be honest without scaring her. When my husband overheard me one day, he nodded. It was a "that's my story and I'm sticking to it" kind of tacit agreement.

Nana, having lived a lot longer, is much more relaxed about this.

Juliette and I saw a dog and stopped to pet it. Juliette explained that she had a cat in Heaven and next year she would like to get a dog. Our chats about death are simple and important. Children who cannot discuss death become less free with their emotions. I've taken advantage of Juliette's curiosity by mentioning the possibility of my death. I asked Juliette to wear a cheerful yellow dress and carry flowers. Now Juliette can focus on my request rather than her fear of losing me. The funeral will feel more comfortable as a celebration of life.

The death of our loved ones is a horrible loss, but you can make it easier. You can give your grandchildren perspective on another family member's passing by comparing how flowers grow and die and how some insects are born and die in the same day. You can give your grandchildren a warm feeling to keep forever when it is your time. After all, you'll be watching them from Heaven.

Memorabilia

Open the attic to your grandchildren. That old chest full of treasure holds just as much magic for your grandchildren as it does for you. You can explain to the children how you found that lucky rabbit's foot and tell them about the dance when you wore those stained white gloves. Show them the locket your first boyfriend gave you and let them play dress-up in your old mink stole. If your grandchild seems particularly attached to your faded horseback riding ribbon, give it to him outright as a keepsake or put it aside for a special gift later.

Let the children into your life by sharing things that were a part of it. Be a part of their lives by collecting items that are meaningful to all of you and designating them as your time capsule. A squirt gun that won't be missed, a baby tooth, a souvenir program, and a calendar page saved in a shoe box will bring laughs and happy memories a few years from now. Perhaps you'd like to use a coffee can and bury it in the yard. You could make it into a big event by agreeing on a special date to open the time capsule. Memorabilia is not junk—it's history you can touch!

Create Loving Memories

Most of our earliest memories are vital ones, whether positive or negative. It follows that your memories of grandma are emotional, as well. My mother remembers her grandma carrying her down the attic stairs during a house fire. Her sister distinctly remembers her grandma *not* carrying her out of the house. Grandmas can't be everywhere all the time. Be conscious of creating happy memories for your grandchildren not only to remember you by, but also to use as fodder for their own grandparenting styles.

I often visualize my grandchild telling her children stories about our happy times together. When I buy tickets to the "Nutcracker", I smile to myself as I imagine Juliette recounting our annual trips to the ballet.

Memories of you will make your grandchildren feel loved . . . and feel love for you.

Die Happy

After several months, my friend Donna finally gathered the courage to visit her Grandmother's grave. She became very upset when she saw the words "Mother" and "Wife" carved on the headstone. Immediately, she went to the stone mason and demanded that the title "Grandmother" be added. It was more than justice, she felt. It was the highest tribute.

Many people feel that once they have grandchildren, their job on Earth is truly done. They've lived their life, so whatever happens is okay. They can "die happy". (Great grandchildren are an extra bonus.)

Since I've become a grandma, I'm more aware that Heaven is the next step in the life cycle. And I don't mind, because now I've got Heaven on Earth.

The Circle of Life

You can give your grandchildren a sense of continuity by reminiscing about the past and dreaming about the future. Remind them that someday, if they are very lucky, they will be grandparents, too.

You know you're a member of Club Grandma when . . .

— you know the names of all the characters on "Sesame Street."

— you have fingerprints below your door-knobs.

— you volunteer to baby-sit.

— your favorite bedmate is your grand-daughter.

— you feel warm all over.

CLUB GRANDMA
Handbook for Happiness

Resources

Grandmothers for Peace International
Director: Barbara Weidner
9444 Medstead
Elk Grove, CA 95758
(916)684-0394

R. F. D. Travel Corporation, "Grandparents & Grandchildren"
5201 Johnson Drive
Mission, KS 66205
1-800-365-5359

Today's Young Grandparents Club
Director: Sunie Levin
P.O. Box 11143
Shawnee Mission, KS 66207
(913)642-8296

GRANDMAS ARE TO LOVE